PERSONAL PRESENCE

HOW SPEAKERS
AUTHENTICALLY ENGAGE

To my dear daughter Hannah who understands

Personal presence: how speakers authentically engage

Every possible effort has been made to ensure that the information contained in this publication is accurate at the time of going to press. Neither the publisher nor the author can accept responsibility for any errors or omissions, however caused. Nor can any responsibility be accepted for loss or damage as a result of reading this publication.

Published by Novaro Publishing Ltd, Techno Park, Coventry University Technology Park, Puma Way, Coventry CV1 2TT
e: publish@novaropublishing.com.

© Sarah Thurstan, 2020

The right of Sarah Thurstan to be identified as the author of this publication has been asserted by them in accordance with the Copyright, Design and Patents Act 1988.

All rights reserved. Apart from any fair dealing for the purposes of research or private study, criticism or review, this publication may only be reproduced, stored or transmitted in any form or by any means with the prior permission in writing of the publisher.

ISBN: 978-1-9998329-8-8
E-ISBN: 978-1-9998329-9-5

British Library Cataloguing-in-Publication Data
A catalogue record for this book is available from the British Library.

Designed by Chantel Barnett, Clear Design CC Ltd.

For further details about our authors and our titles, see
www.novaropublishing.com.

PERSONAL PRESENCE

HOW SPEAKERS AUTHENTICALLY ENGAGE

SARAH THURSTAN

ABOUT THE AUTHOR

Sarah Thurstan has helped hundreds of speakers get their big moments right in front of a live audience. She coaches leaders, professionals and influencers on how to speak authentically in public and engage their audiences, whether it's a one-minute pep talk, an interview on camera or a presentation at an industry event. Drawing on her years of experience as an actress in theatre and film, including roles on the BBC's Silent Witness and ITV's Coronation Street, she develops everyone's unique speaking style, bringing their strengths, their values and their stories to the fore. As a coach, she has helped executives from many organizations, including a global bank and a national police force, to find their authentic voice and perform as their natural selves in public. She is a director of Performance Link, a company that specializes in developing a speaker's personal presence and making them feel comfortable in their own skin about the whole experience of performing.

CONTENTS

Foreword
Frances and Kathryn Nichols, The Nichols Group   vii

Introduction   1

1. What is personal presence?   6
2. Playing to our strengths   13
3. Fighting the fear   26
4. Physical communication   36
5. Storytelling   53
6. Engaging your audience   63
7. Lessons from the Greeks: rule of three   77
8. Structure   83
9. Self-awareness, self-disclosure and self-confidence   92
10. Elevator pitches and talking to camera   100
11. Diction, delivery and jargon   106

12.	Directions and props	112
13.	Performing as a leader	123
14.	Business theatre	130
15.	Cornerstones and competence	139

Appendices

1.	Ten inspiring articles, talks and ideas	151
2.	Warm-up routines	154

Acknowledgements 157

FOREWORD

Communication is everything. It is how we connect with each other and see each other. The business world thrives and fails on communication. Good communication is the route of all successful relationships and poor communication is the basis of relationship breakdowns.

As change specialists at Nichols, we turn vision to reality on major programmes to build a better future and, as creative specialists, we drive transformational ideas to raise business consciousness. We have been working with Sarah for 20 years and during that time she has presented her course on personal presence to all of our people. She has always received glowing reviews.

There are always some who enjoy speaking out and find it easy to present. However, many more do not enjoy it and find it most intimidating. Speaking in a group can be challenging. It involves stepping into the unknown. It involves risk. When one presents, you are being seen showing and sharing something of yourself. Often you may not know the people you are presenting to; it can be daunting and you may feel vulnerable. As individuals, we fear negative reactions and don't want to look stupid in front of others.

A successful presentation can make you feel good, uplifted, inspired. People will remember it for a long time afterwards and your message will have been heard. Good presentations include awareness of your audience and the mood in the room. Sarah has a gift for teaching us how to bring out our own authentic voice and the confidence to deliver our messages.

She makes you look at things in a totally different way. Clarity of message. The power of three. Self-belief. Who is the audience? What message do you want to share? What do you want them to remember? Sarah works on your positive attributes, on what you do well. This is most refreshing and builds your confidence. Therefore, you can relax and enjoy presenting much more. We have found that Sarah's practical feedback highlights your strengths and identifies how to improve in order to create better presentations.

Tone, physicality, and the power of the visual are vitally important when storytelling and creating the right energy in the room. This has helped us go from reluctant speakers to enjoying presenting, focusing on our messages and even having fun.

FOREWORD

Sarah's book is an excellent guide, not only for presenting well, but for enjoying the experience at the same time. Her book will inspire you to break down presentations into bite-size pieces with a clear path to achieving success. It is always a privilege to work with Sarah and we wholeheartedly recommend her book.

FRANCES AND KATHRYN NICHOLS
Directors, owners and sisters, The Nichols Group

INTRODUCTION

'Orators are made, not born.'

Cicero

It's hard work to become a good speaker. After more than 20 years of work as a professional actress, teacher and as director of Performance Link, I am still amazed that some people think you either have it or you don't, that knack to engaging public speaking. It isn't a knack, it's learning to be your natural self when speaking, coupled with work and practice.

How many times have you seen someone speaking on stage and thought, 'wow, they're impressive. They're a natural.'? Somehow, they truly engage you, their message is clear and memorable, their presence authentic and endearing.

Of course, you'll have probably sat through just as many (if not more) lacklustre, muddled or awkward presentations where you've left mourning those minutes of your life you'll never get back.

If you're reading this book, you're taking a significant step towards becoming that first example. Because believe me, those impressive individuals did not just roll out of bed one day and effortlessly deliver the talk of their lives. They will have worked for it, probably over months or years, and certainly experienced more than their fair share of testing and disheartening episodes.

Perhaps you are already a seasoned pitcher, presenter, performer or public speaker, simply looking for some growth and polish. Wonderful, please read on. Or perhaps, like the vast majority of us, the thought of public speaking remains a terrifying prospect to be avoided at all costs. You are also in the right place, as sooner or later, public speak you must.

In one form or another, the need to be able to stand up and say something in front of some people will arise. And wouldn't you love to be able to spread your ideas, win over clients, colleagues and friends, be an influencer in your profession, do justice to a loved one's eulogy or bring the house down with that perfect wedding speech? Not only is avoiding all forms of public speaking impractical and improbable, but to do so would be to miss out on something deeply powerful.

INTRODUCTION

Even in a world pervaded by cutting-edge communications technology, the uniquely human ability to connect face to face with other people remains highly prized, not least in the increasingly competitive sphere of business. If you master the skill of presenting, it will reward you with meaningful progress wherever you apply it. When I say the skill of presenting, what I really mean is the power of communication. So what is it exactly?

It is the power to express, to inspire, to influence, to educate, to excite, to question, to connect. In this book, I will talk about how this personal power lies within all of us and can be nurtured into fruition through a series of simple techniques and guided personal insights. My intention is that this book will help you both as a presenter, but also as a person in your day-to-day life. My signature programme for Performance Link is called Personal Presence and I think this sums up what I would like you to gain by reading this book. I hope it will lead you down roads of personal development, as well as acting as a practical guide for those times you need concrete support.

We all have our stories to tell. Sharpening our self-awareness and sharing them with authenticity is what I have learned really matters.

It's been a long and colourful road which has led me to write this book. I'll share with you just a few snapshots from this journey and from what sometimes feels like past lives. I used to teach English in a Finnish paper and pulp company in the Arctic Circle. I learned circus skills with the renowned Como brothers of Amsterdam, played the gong slave in Oscar Wilde's *Salome* in Belgium, and toured Holland with experimental theatre company KISS. In the mid 1980s, personal circumstances took me abruptly from performing in London's West End to running an open-all-hours shop on a council estate in Cumbria with my two-week-old baby, who, truth be told, didn't really pull her weight. I remember my attempts to introduce French cheese and paté at the cold counter were greeted with particular bafflement and disdain by the locals. I taught for some time at a specialist school for boys with severe behavioural difficulties — now that was a tough audience. I've presented in Washington to a hundred vice-presidents from blue-chip companies and coached Swiss Bank wealth managers on their executive presence.

Looking back, it's apparent to me that the threads that tie all of these seemingly incongruous experiences together are people and connections. Whoever the audience, whatever my role or relationship to them, expressing myself effectually was essential, and always boiled down to the same three fundamentals: authenticity, storytelling and self-awareness. I will talk about these three cornerstones of

INTRODUCTION

communication in more detail throughout the book. For now, I thank you for reading and wish you every success in strengthening your own command of communication. May you enjoy confidence and growth in all areas of your life.

1.
WHAT IS PERSONAL PRESENCE?

'Everyone has their own ways of expression. I believe we all have a lot to say, but finding ways to say it is more than half the battle.'

Criss Jami

Personal presence is an expression of your true self. It sums up the value of who you are, your behaviour, your ethos, your look and voice. It is how you communicate and connect with the world, and how the world sees you. That connection can only be made when we are being authentic.

In our day-to-day lives, most of us are doing this every day all the time without thinking. But once asked to stand up in front of people and speak publicly, we often struggle

WHAT IS PERSONAL PRESENCE?

to maintain our personal presence which could also be described as our authentic voice.

Imagine sitting around the dinner table with your friends having an impassioned discussion on the environment. Your ideas and opinions flow effortlessly. You speak in the moment and respond without hesitation, you are yourself, you feel relaxed and are having fun. Now imagine you are asked to deliver a 15-minute presentation on the environment to an audience of a hundred people. How do you feel?

If you're like most people, that natural ease of expression probably just goes out of the window. To express ourselves confidently and naturally, without looking nervous, without suffering blanks, without shaking, stammering or sweating, isn't straightforward. It requires work, even for those who may appear to be excellent off-the-cuff speakers.

Why is this important in business? Your authentic voice can be seen when delivering a sales pitch, motivational team talk, keynote speech, educational lecture or a plea to your company — the list goes on.

Allow me to tell you a story. After the privatization of the railways in 1991, Britain suffered five major rail disasters. One of these happened at Potters Bar and is included in David Hare's magnificent play *The Permanent Way*. Two people known to me, Nina Bawden and her husband Austen

Kark, were on that train. Austen died and Nina suffered serious injuries from which she never quite recovered. Some friends of Nina's were travelling to Austen's memorial service in a taxi and the driver noted that the bells of St Martin's were pealing out over Trafalgar Square. They told the driver that the bells were for their friend who had died in the Potters Bar rail disaster. The taxi driver turned off his meter, saying, 'it's the least I can do'.

'They know, you see. People know,' says David Hare as a comment. The reason I tell this story is that humanity and compassion are within us all, and even a brief interaction with a stranger can be a moment of connection. That gesture of the taxi driver clearly expresses his attitude, ethos and behaviours, his sensitivity to the significance of the event. Those few words coupled with his generous action are his personal presence.

Authenticity is key. People trust natural people. Being fully present and comfortable so that your authentic self shines through, as if you were talking to a single friend, even in an auditorium of a thousand is the secret of success. Telling the truth and speaking wholeheartedly with passion will win you rapport and engagement. Facts and figures are often secondary.

I work regularly with people from different companies on their personal presence. We build on their self-awareness, focus on their strengths and learn the tools to better their communication skills. They have two days to concentrate on themselves, on who they are and how the world views them. It is often a light-bulb moment, as they have rarely had time to think carefully about how they express themselves. Yet it is so important that they know exactly how they appear to different audiences, so they can be their most effective in meeting expectations.

'It's not what we know, but how we choose to communicate what we know that really counts.'

Jonathan Stevens, senior consultant,
Impact International

Owning your presentation

Everybody must have ownership of their presentation. To begin, this means scripting it ourselves. Including ideas, quotes or data from external sources is absolutely fine, and input and feedback from friends or colleagues is welcomed, but the body of what we are saying must be original — in our own words and tone of voice. Whether it's a team review, pitching a new product, presenting marketing analysis or teaching your students a new concept, you want to have a sound knowledge and understanding of what it is you are talking about. Just as a wedding speech would fall flat if given by someone who has never actually met the newlyweds, it is ill advised to stand up and try to inform at length about a subject or experience that you can't talk about with honesty and proficiency. It may sometimes mean doing a little extra homework, but it will give you the best chance of feeling comfortable and confident on the day.

Perhaps a colleague falls ill, and you find yourself being asked last minute by a manager to deliver someone else's presentation for them. Alarm bells. Please don't agree. Have the courage to say politely: 'No, sorry but I can do *my* presentation'.

Being handed a memory stick with 30 slides the night before is not acceptable. You will not be able to be sincere or have credibility in this situation. Best to do your own version from scratch or a version of what they have done that makes you feel more knowledgeable and comfortable.

It's important to have belief in your message and deliver it with conviction and authenticity. Not only does this give you vital credibility in your audience's eyes, but it will also make life much easier for you when it comes to the delivery. With ownership of your content you can enjoy increased confidence and fewer nerves. If you have memorized your presentation well but still suffer a blank, you will recover much more quickly and calmly if you are able to draw from your knowledge and simply talk about the subject in your own language.

Politicians are an example of why ownership matters. One of the reasons they often come over as so insincere is because they have speechwriters. You will notice that at the beginning of their careers they appear more authentic and endearing when they are still expressing themselves in their own words. They speak wholeheartedly as if in a one-to-one conversation with their best friend. Whatever your politics, it certainly proved a key turning point for David Cameron's leadership bid back in 2005. During the speech he gave at the Conservative party conference, knowing he was trailing David Davis in the leadership race, he stepped away from the lectern completely and spoke without notes and with great passion. His delivery had such a candour and natural ease that he received a three-minute standing ovation from party representatives. No one had even heard of him before that. Ultimately, he won twice as many votes as Davis, whose campaign was said to have been marred by a poor conference speech.

PERSONAL PRESENCE

'If you celebrate your differentness, the world will too. It believes exactly what you tell it through the words you use to describe yourself, the actions you take to care for yourself and the choices you make to express yourself.'

Victoria Moran

2.
PLAYING TO OUR STRENGTHS

'To become conscious and aware, we must become authentic. Authenticity is the highest form of being.'
Teal Swan

'Knowing yourself is the beginning of all wisdom.'
Aristotle

I believe that every one of us has natural communication strengths and that it is on these strengths we must always concentrate and build, not on our weaknesses. These days this natural quality is known as authenticity. Yes, there will be areas we can work on, but better to put our best foot forward and lead with the qualities we innately command.

For example, is smiling a powerful and endearing characteristic when speaking? Absolutely. Should former prime minister Gordon Brown (probably under ill advice) have forced unnatural grins whilst on television? Probably not. It simply didn't come naturally to him in those situations and thus came across as insincere. Far from having the desired effect of appearing more relatable to the public, it actually turned people off further. John Prescott even dubbed it, albeit rather harshly, 'the worst smile in the world'. Sincerity is crucial. As Oscar Wilde rightly said, 'be yourself, everyone else is taken'.

It is a markedly British tendency to often note the negative in someone's efforts before the good. It seems to be our way of not allowing our children or those nearest to us to become big headed or arrogant. Modesty and self-deprecating humour are what is considered acceptable. Many of us go through life having our mistakes and shortcomings pointed out to us by those around us. I remember the red face and discomfort of my friend's teenage son as his report card was read aloud to the entire family one year. He was publicly chastised for getting a D in French, despite achieving straight As in almost every other subject, including chemistry and maths.

In fact, research reveals that it is a common behaviour. Many parents tend to read the low grades or the adverse comments in a school report before congratulating their child on improvements or areas of triumph.

PLAYING TO OUR STRENGTHS

Geoffrey Banks, a talented actor from Bolton I once knew, won a scholarship to Cambridge to study languages, where he became involved in the crafty magical arts of theatre. Due to the responsibilities of supporting a wife and children after the second world war, he never progressed to being a professional actor until he retired at 60. He instead worked most of his life at a boys' school teaching French and German, but on the weekends, he recorded for BBC Radio 4 and then one year was cast in an amateur production of Hamlet at Bolton Little Theatre. After a draining eight-hour school day, he would go to perform in the theatre. One night his mother was in the audience. After a sterling performance, he asked her, 'what did you think?', to which she replied simply in her Boltonian accent, after looking him up and down, 'eee, you were thin'.

What his being slim had to do with the show was, of course, irrelevant, but it again highlights the British reluctance to offer sincere, positive praise and the quickness many of us have to pick on any negatives. This mentality is so prolific in our culture that not only do we struggle to give meaningful praise to others, but most of us are also uncomfortable receiving it. In contrast, in the US it is common for adults to praise children and themselves with pats on the back and effusive compliments, something we would probably find cringe-making or even improper.

Whilst at times the unbridled positivity can seem to veer on the side of saccharine or insincere, there is a valuable lesson in their sunny, cheerleader attitude for us more cynical Brits. It is important we focus on the positives and offer genuine praise and encouragement to those around us.

Physical and character strengths

When trying to discern both ours and others' strengths in communication, we can think about them in two categories: physical and character.

Physical strengths are the bodily attributes others may perceive upon meeting you for the first time. They don't need to know you. These strengths are visible, audible and palpable. They include assertive eye contact, centred posture, a warm smiling face, a positive energy, open body language, a soothing tone or clear diction. Note that these are distinct from plain physical features, for example a shapely nose or long-flowing hair, which don't really tell us anything meaningful about the person's presence and strengths in communication.

Character strengths are those associated with personal values: our beliefs, philosophies and actions. They relate to how we view the world and operate within it. Some examples would be honesty, approachability, commitment, integrity, humility, intelligence, resilience and, of course, a sense of humour.

So how do we know what our physical and character strengths are? We ask people. It seems absurdly simple, even obvious, and yet asking others for targeted feedback is something few of us do. Perhaps the need to ask simply hasn't occurred to us before. Or we're unsure who to ask. For some of us it is because we're fearful of what we might hear. What if they can't think of anything positive to say? Fear not, they always can.

The people around us are uniquely positioned to provide a window onto our communication style. After all, you can only take part in any interaction as yourself and it is impossible to experience yourself through another person's eyes and experiences. In other words, the only way to truly know how you come across to others, is if other people tell you. Waiting for these precious words to wash upon us though is foolhardy. Who has the time? If we are seriously looking to develop and grow, we need to kickstart the process by actively inviting constructive feedback. Feedback is a gift.

The art of feedback

When it comes to giving feedback, a good rule is to try to

always begin with a positive and end with a positive. People naturally react to the first thing they hear: encouragement and praise help to set the tone, disarm potential defensiveness and give the listener the confidence and reassurance to receive any constructive feedback that follows.

Studies in behavioural science also show us that our memory of an experience is most vividly coloured by how it ends. So, in a conversational setting, the last comments we hear will be those most likely to have lasting resonance. Therefore, also ending on a high note will leave your colleague or friend with a positive lasting impression. With this they will feel buoyed and more motivated to work on any feedback discussed.

I'll share with you a time when I experienced the impact of how we frame our words. My actress colleague Sue and I were asked to perform at a conference in Harrogate for the North West E-Government Group. Sue had scripted an amusing piece about the struggles that the public face in getting through to the county council to complain about lack of lighting in their street, microwaves dumped in back gardens or potholes in the road. A junior government minister had been invited to introduce us. The conference consisted of numerous stalls around which people were milling about and chatting with tannoys on full blast. In order to cut through the crowd's chatter and draw their focus, the minister was briefed to raise his voice and bring people to listen to our sketch. However, as he was rather young and a little shy, he didn't project his voice or direct his attention to people passing. As a result, the room was still far from attentive as we began the piece. Sue and I had to strain our voices during the sketch to get people to stop and listen. After the show, the junior minister asked for some feedback on how his introduction had been. I immediately said without thinking: 'oh, you weren't loud enough, so nobody stopped, but what you said was fine'.

He shrunk a little, immediately looked at his watch and excused himself saying he had to catch the next train back to London. He had been due to introduce us four more times through the course of the day, but my feedback had upset him. He'd tried something out of his comfort zone and the delivery of my feedback had hindered, instead of helped, his confidence during a vulnerable moment. What I should have said was: 'what you said was really good and to the point and next time a little louder'.

In that statement, I have put the positive at the front and the constructive feedback later. I have also joined the two statements with the word 'and' and not 'but'. The word 'but' immediately implies negativity. This was a great learning for me about how to deliver feedback that makes it acceptable for the listener.

Quite often when I work with assertive senior consultants, they always want to know the buts. In reality, if you just gave them a series of negative comments without any positives, they would lose their confidence. It is human nature.

Now, what about getting your feedback? Having decided that you'd like an outside view, from where do you get it?

Well, let's first consider the bank of feedback we each already have. I'm referring to that long list of (often uninvited) comments, observations and opinions about you that various people have voiced over the years. We could call this quantity feedback, as there is a lot of it from a lot of different people.

The value to be found in this type of feedback is that if enough people around us are giving us the same message, it probably has some truth in it and deserves our attention. It's worth remembering though that generally people give too much feedback, because that is what they think they should be doing, especially in a work environment. They are not always thinking of the person that is receiving the feedback and often speak only from their own point of view as they find it difficult to be objective.

For example, an employer who is particularly data driven may comment to an employee that they are 'fluffy' or 'woolly' because they have included emotional reactions in their work. Beware using pejorative words towards others and if on the receiving end, don't take it personally.

The real gold lies in quality feedback. These are the considered and genuinely constructive insights that we receive from trusted individuals. This is what we must actively invite. By asking focused questions and remaining genuinely open to hearing the answers, we lay the groundwork for some valuable self-learning. Choosing who to ask should be done wisely though. Don't just look for people you think will tell you what you want to hear. Equally, be careful not to ask those you see as being unaware of themselves or self-absorbed. Seek out those you trust, whose judgement you respect and feel is fair. People who think of others and will be caring in how they deliver the message, whilst having the confidence, credibility and intuition to give constructive criticism. These are our allies. Engage with them and learn from them.

From the positive feedback we can draw confidence in hearing our strengths affirmed. Any areas highlighted as lacking, are opportunities for personal growth to which we can now give our attention.

'When you talk, words, feelings and body must be in harmony. To achieve this harmony, you must first examine how you feel. Express those feelings through your words, tone of voice and body language.'

Virginia Satir, psychologist and educator

Test your strengths

Physical strengths

Choose a physical strength you have. For example, 'I've been told I have good eye contact'. Now unpack it. Ask, what exactly is this strength? Write down with a pen and paper what it does (or doesn't) look like. So how could we define good eye contact?

- Gently holding someone's gaze for two to three seconds in a group or presentation setting, or for longer if talking one on one.

- Not unfocused, side-to-side, tennis-match eye contact.

- Not shifty eyes, darting up and down too much.

- Not over focusing with wide eyes or furrowed brow that can feel too intense.

What does this strength say about someone? What can we read from that person when they make good eye contact?

- They are an active listener.

- They are focused.

- They are present.

- They are acknowledging me.

Character strengths

Choose a character strength you have. For example, 'I am a fair person who strongly believes in equality'. Character strengths could be loyalty, trustworthiness, fair-mindedness, sense of humour, approachability, credibility, integrity, family values, commitment, hardworking, humility and so on. Now unpack this quality. How does it show itself physically?

For example, somebody that believes in being an approachable and accessible person, will often be somebody who smiles and shows warmth through open body language. People who have an innate curiosity in others will also reveal that physically. If you are a calm person it will show in your physical demeanour by the way you don't fidget a lot and sit still, which makes those around you feel relaxed and at ease. Also, if you really believe in something your enthusiasm will shine through when you speak, often with gestures, bright active eyes and a more dynamic pace and tone of voice. People will be engaged and want to listen.

'Nothing great was achieved without enthusiasm.'

Ralph Waldo Emerson

Feedback on strengths

Your next task is to ask a colleague what strengths they have seen in you, again, one physical and one character. Now you are asking someone else for targeted, quality feedback. Having decided who that trusted person will be, invite their comments on a one-on-one basis with an open mind.

Once armed with quality feedback, our self-awareness

grows. We can now solidly identify our communication strengths, and this builds our confidence. I recommend writing down your strengths in a workbook or journal, so they are always available as a reminder. In times of fear and challenge, it is good to remember our toolbox of strengths and keep them at the front of our thinking, for example, when faced with an audience or a difficult client meeting.

'To thine own self be true.'

William Shakespeare

3.
FIGHTING THE FEAR

'According to most studies, the average person's number one fear is public speaking ... number two is death.'

Jerry Seinfeld

A friend once got me a great last-minute audition at the Royal Exchange Theatre, Manchester. My father had just passed away and I'd hurriedly flown back from France. I was in an emotionally fragile state and hideously underprepared. I wasn't feeling good. When I got out on stage, before I even started speaking, I felt my right leg begin to tremble, the aggressive vibration of a trapped nerve. Instead of taking a moment to shake it out and breathe, anxiously I forged ahead with the audition, but my attention was so diverted by my leg, which was now violently wobbling, that my performance was distracted and unfeeling. Needless to say, I didn't get the part.

FIGHTING THE FEAR

We can all relate to experiencing intense nerves at some point, especially before public speaking. One woman I worked with, Lisa, said this:

> When I started at Nichols, public speaking would make me physically shake, make me feel like my voice was wobbling and breaking. I would get those feelings you get before you faint, where everything goes a bit quiet and dark and time goes by in a blur. My main goal was to 'survive it' and the concept of actually enjoying it was laughable. I would never volunteer to speak and would be inclined to say no if asked. It was an ordeal.

Perhaps you can relate? But why is it that we all suffer from stage fright? And what are the main symptoms of this particular brand of fear? You may recognise some of these common ones: dry mouth, a 'washing machine' stomach, clammy hands, a restricted throat, shaky voice, sweating or the shakes.

Psychologists have examined the question of what it is that makes us so frightened of public speaking. Do we fear we will look foolish? Or that we will let others and ourselves down? In short, we fear rejection from the social group. In this moment of self-exposure and extreme vulnerability, a primal fear kicks in and chemicals flood the body. The sensation is beyond that of everyday embarrassment or mere judgement. It is a visceral and subconscious fear of being ostracized if we make a mistake and it can be traced back to our ancestors' times, when expulsion from the tribe into the wilds really did spell a death sentence. Though the fear of failure in our society is as strong as ever, happily, we have evolved somewhat and it is unlikely that you'll be banished to wander the icy nether regions alone simply for blanking in a meeting or stammering in a pitch.

Yet our bodies try to trick us into feeling it is still a matter of life or death. The fight or flight response is triggered and what was once a useful adrenaline kick for our hunter-gatherer ancestors seems, in today's world, like a cruel flaw that can feel insurmountable when faced with an expectant audience.

There's good news though: by facing this fear and practising several proven techniques, it is absolutely possible to calm our nerves, banish those negative thoughts and conquer our stage fright.

We can also take comfort in knowing that everybody suffers from these fears, even those we least expect, who seem confident and self-assured in their public speaking and performance.

From my years on stage and coaching many professionals, I've picked up some useful techniques to help you combat this fear and quiet the busy mind of anxiety and concern. By clearing the mind using these exercises, whilst preparing the body and voice to present, your focus will be sharper, and you will bring control and balance back into your delivery.

Six tips to conquer stage fright

Prepare

The more prepared you are, the less room there is for fear. So rehearse, rehearse and rehearse. When you deliver your presentation, you don't want to be worrying about the contents or whether the visual aids are in the right order, so get prepared ahead of time. Record yourself on your phone and listen to it back before bedtime to help it sink into your unconscious. Do a workshop – anything to keep practising and help the presentation become second nature and embedded. The more comfortable and familiar you are with your content, the more relaxed you will feel on the day.

Imagine it

Just as you can imagine a disaster, so too can you create positive mental pictures. For a week before the big event and particularly before going to sleep, imagine yourself performing brilliantly. Literally see yourself doing it well. Allow yourself to play with the image, exaggerating how wonderful it might be. Picture yourself as a star performer and feel the audience's approving reactions. Since your mind will be creating anticipatory images anyway, you may as well make them positive ones, rather than nightmares. Wilfully re-channel your energy from being nervous about what could go wrong. Instead, allow yourself to feel excited about everything that could go right.

Rest and relaxation

Try not to burn yourself out in the lead-up to your presentation and get a good night's sleep the night before. Exercising helps to clear the mind and wear out the body. Or why not try soaking in a hot bath, drinking chamomile tea, listening to a comforting podcast or reading an inspiring book? I recommend doing some breathing relaxation exercises (see below). If you are lying in bed still wide awake, then try systematically tensing up the muscles in each part of your body one by one. Clench and release three times over, working from the toes right up to your face to help tire you out and relax the body and mind. Another useful trick, if you can't sleep due to worry, can be to write down your fears on paper. Dump them all out of your mind and onto the page, then in the morning, tear up or burn the paper and face the day.

Reframe it

Many of the same fright symptoms occur when we are excited, in anticipation, or attracted to someone. Think about the dry mouth and butterflies we experience when falling in love. Telling yourself you are nervous merely reinforces fear. Instead, try to change the internal dialogue and remind yourself that you are excited. That's why you're short of breath and your knees have gone wobbly. If a negative projection starts to play out in your mind, try to notice it and nip it in the bud by reminding yourself of the excitement of possibility. Try cultivating a feeling of gratitude for this opportunity, which, no matter the outcome, opens up the possibility for personal growth and learning. Feel proud and emboldened by your own badass bravery.

Limber

Before a presentation, we need to channel the energy that is rushing through our bodies. A vigorous shake-out, followed by some relaxed, steady nasal breathing will help. Before taking centre stage, be sure to actually use your voice so it too has a chance to warm up. See below for some exercises for this.

Stop

Before launching into your presentation, stop. We call this the presenter's highway code: stop, look, listen, breath and start. This allows you to arrive in front of your audience. It slows you down, preventing you from gabbling. Steadying your breathing helps to steady your voice. Just as you have allowed a pause at the beginning before you start, in exactly the same way allow a pause at the end when you have finished speaking. Don't run away immediately. Imagine you have listened to a concert and as the last notes of the symphony die away, the audience remains quiet and in that hush you feel the final vibrations of the music, then the clapping comes. Hold the moment for at least three seconds before breaking the spell and magic of your presentation.

FIGHTING THE FEAR

Exercises: ready the body and voice

Do these exercises shortly before you are due to talk:

- With knees hip-distance apart, flop over on soft knees, let your head hang loose, arms trailing to the ground. Rest here a moment.

- Breath out as much as you can expelling every last bit of air from your lungs, breathe in deeply.

- Come up slowly, vertebra by vertebra, breathing out, head last. Roll shoulders back and down as if almost making the shoulder blades touch with an open chest, then into a grounded standing position with a neutral stance, hands by your side. Relaxed.

- Stand up tall. Imagine a string pulling up from your crown lifting your head up.

- Yawn widely to open the throat and clear the sinuses.

- Massage the face with two fingers in small circular movements.

- Stretch your face, pull all facial muscles forwards and backwards.

- Squeeze eyes together as tightly as possible then open them. Repeat three times.

- Take three deep breaths expanding your rib cage and diaphragm outwards. Use your hands to feel the expansion as if your rib cage is a pair of bellows: squeeze your ribs inwards as you exhale. Count to 10, then 15 and 20, building your capacity on your exhalation of each breath.

- Hum deeply to open your throat and resonators. Feel the vibrations. The vibration is the resonance your body is creating. Pay attention to the sensations and vibrations all over your face, temples, forehead, side of the nose, top of chest, shoulders, back and top of the head. The more you can feel, the more the sound will increase and vibrate.

Then on one breath repeat these tongue-twisters three times each:

FIGHTING THE FEAR

- Gloria Groot glued a groat to Gregory's goat.

- A bloke's back brake block broke.

- A thin little boy picked six thick thistle sticks.

- Of all the felt I ever felt, I never felt a piece of felt, which felt as fine as that felt felt, when first I felt that felt hat's felt.

To use an analogy, your body is like a violin. The strings are your vocal chords found in the dip at the base of your throat. Your muscles, tendons and bone are the sounding board of your body, which gives resonance to your sound and texture to your pitch. Finally, your breath is the bow of the violin.

All three parts need to flow and if you concentrate on these elements in your warm-up, your nerves will slowly wane and disappear. All of this will help you fight the fear and look as confident as those speakers you seek to emulate.

4.
PHYSICAL COMMUNICATION

'Your body language, your eyes, your energy will come through to your audience before you even start speaking.'

Peter Guber

I was teaching a group workshop for a large, well-known bank. The employees were a collection of bright, confident youngsters fresh from university. During the first session, with us all gathered in a circle, one young man quickly made his presence felt. He sat splayed on his chair, chest puffed out, legs wide apart, with one arm draped over the back of the girl's chair next to him. He seemed unaware of the message he was physically transmitting to the room. Rather than pull him up on it publicly and embarrass him, I waited until a little later in the day then copied the pose myself and asked the group what they thought of this posture. Everyone agreed, and the girls in particular commented, that it conveyed arrogance, possession, overconfidence, disrespect and a need to show who's top dog. Hopefully he picked up on the message.

What we say with our bodies matters. Body language is universal, it is the language that we all speak whether we realise it or not. Long before we were talking or scratching out the first human alphabets, our hunter-gatherer ancestors were communicating with each other using only the inborn tools of non-verbal communication, tools we all still possess today. Body language is the first language that we respond to as babies. The reassuring closeness and softness of touch from a mother brings us safety and comfort. A warm, vigilant gaze from a parent to their child's eyes builds connection and forges deep emotional bonds. Think of all the grinning faces, exaggerated expressions and jovial, babbling vocal tones that we instinctively use around babies to try to make them laugh and bring them joy. Or the crying that ensues when toddlers see their parents arguing aggressively. They cannot yet comprehend the words or their meanings, but the raised volume and pitch, furrowed brows and hostile gestures tell them instinctively that something is wrong. Babies feel intention, and so do we.

Negative body languague is mainly due to old habits, a lack of self-awareness or a behavioural response to feeling out of our comfort zone. These are areas we can work on to build new habits and responses, ones that will allow our authentic and relaxed self to shine through. I will share some exercises to help with this further on in the chapter.

What exactly is body language?

Body language or, more broadly, non-verbal communication, is simply communication without using words. It is the information we pick up on irrelevant of what someone is actually saying, if indeed they're even speaking at all.

For example, an open, flat hand gesturing silently towards somebody signifies an invitation, inclusion, referencing or even a sharing. However, a pointed finger towards a person tells them they are wrong, a target or being reprimanded; it is reminiscent of something negative, like being scolded by a teacher at school. You'd be surprised just how much information can be discerned from these physical cues:

- Facial expressions
- Smiling
- Eye contact
- Gestures
- Visual pictures
- Posture
- Tone of voice

- Volume of voice
- Musicality or intonation of voice
- Rate of speech (pace)
- Diction
- Vocal inflection
- Physical appearance
- Touch
- Use of space
- Personal grooming
- Pitch
- Stillness and calm
- Energy and presence

Let's try out our own powers of perception. Picture a scene of a man alone in a room. The top button of his shirt is undone, and his tie is slightly loose. His hair is unkempt and he's visibly sweating as he paces the room, eyes cast down, biting his nails and gesticulating erratically. He intermittently clears his throat and takes sips of water with a shaking hand.

Now imagine another scene. A woman sits back in a chair, her legs gently crossed and both hands resting on top of her head with fingers loosely interlaced. Her face is still with eyes lightly closed and the trace of a small smile at the corners of her mouth. Her chest slowly rises as she breathes in deeply through her nose. She opens her eyes and watches out of the window for a while. Her eyes fix on something for a moment then a smile breaks out across her whole face.

Alternatively, imagine you are in a meeting and someone leans far back in their chair and puts their hands on their head with their elbows at 90 degrees, nose in the air and eyes open, and not making eye contact with anybody in the room, usually looking at the ceiling. This stance is common amongst men, often senior male leaders, and even senior female leaders. It can say:

- 'Entertain me'
- 'I am the boss'
- 'What have you got to offer?'

This is an arrogant or over-assertive stance, very different from the previous example of the woman sitting back in a chair with her eyes lightly closed.

What different impressions did these three wordless tableaus give you of their characters? What state of mind do you think they are each in? Did you automatically construct little stories around them? How do you imagine the energy in those three rooms feels?

You can see from these contrasting scenes just how much we perceive emotions and mindset through mere physicality. By the same token, we ourselves are transmitting these signals to others all the time, not least of all when we are public speaking.

Gestures versus visual pictures

One thing many of us naturally do as we express ourselves is to gesticulate. It's a great way to help animate our stories and inject interest into our physicality. Visual pictures are another powerful addition to our arsenal. The difference between a gesture and a visual picture is that a gesture is non-specific. It is a broad or abstract action that can accompany a variety of expressions. A visual picture on the other hand (pun intended) is a deliberate representation of what you are saying, an action that mirrors your speech, paints a clear picture for your audience and makes what you're saying highly memorable.

For example, imagine you're talking about a time you were caught out in the rain. You could create a visual picture of this situation by miming yourself clutching an umbrella with hunched up shoulders. Or if you are listing three important points, you could hold up three fingers to mirror and emphasise this, highly effective at helping an audience absorb what you're saying.

I highly recommend having a go at incorporating some

visual pictures into your presentations. Test their efficacy out with a friendly audience by asking them to tell you which bits of your presentation or story they particularly remembered. It will often be those moments when you coupled your words with a visual picture.

The expression of emotions

Considering the ancient and intrinsic nature of body language, the science of non-verbal communication is a relatively modern field. The great evolutionary biologist Charles Darwin was the first person to study it formally in his 1872 book, *The Expression of the Emotions in Man and Animals*. He observed that humans, like other animals, had a repertoire of innate physical cues that are used to express emotions and communicate. Upon these findings, a wider interest later grew and the study of kinesics was established in the mid 20th century. Kinesics (the study of body language) serves to categorize and understand how different gestures developed and the various meanings they hold in communication.

In his renowned research during the 1970s, Albert Mehrabian, emeritus professor of psychology at UCLA, pinpointed the differences, and relative importance, of visual, vocal and verbal communication during public speaking or whenever you are in the spotlight.

He surmised that how we express ourselves visually, vocally and verbally also reflects our value structure. That is, that when you speak, the intonation of your voice, the tone and speed you use, the gestures you make, and, of course, your posture, body language, eye contact and facial expressions, are all the things people notice first. What we sometimes call first impressions.

The three Vs of communication

Visual

The visual pertains to everything that others see, from how animated your face is, to the degree you use your hands to express yourself, in fact, to every element of your physical being, what we call in general body language. It can also involve your energy or aura, the presence you bring into a room with you non-verbally.

Vocal

This is the how of your speech: the intonation, volume, accent, clarity, diction, pitch and even the timbre of your voice.

Verbal

The actual words that you use. The content of your speech.

Looking at the three Vs above, what percentage would you apportion to these three ways of communication in terms of importance and impact?

Professor Mehrabian's study, *Silent Messages*, asserts that as much as 93 percent of our impact comes from how we look, behave and sound (38 percent vocal and 55 percent visual) while a mere 7 percent comes from the words we actually say.

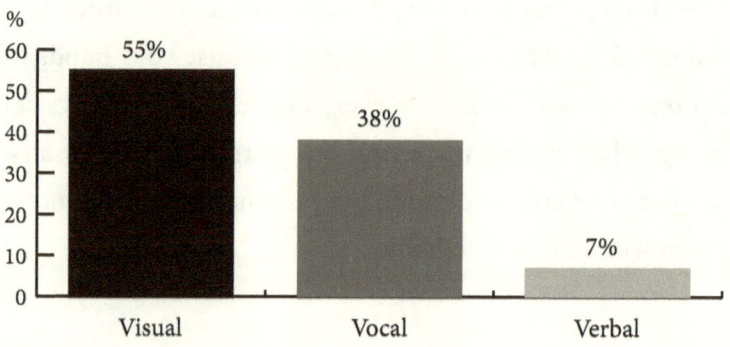

Figure 4.1: The three Vs of communication

Note that this piece of research only appertains to public speaking or a time when you are in the spotlight, not necessarily one to one. Therefore it isn't what you say but the way that you say it. For example if you say, 'I am really excited to be here with you today', whilst looking at the floor (no eye contact), hand touching your nose and standing awkwardly with your weight on one leg, arms crossed (defensive) and unclear speech that is directed downwards, no-one will believe you. On the page they may, but not when you are saying it live, because your visual and your vocal do not match the verbal. As Ella Fitzgerald sings in her song: 't'aint what you say it's the way that you say it'.

When you no longer have the visual because you are on the phone or on a conference call, the vocal, ie, the tone, pitch, emphasis, pace and intonation is 75 percent and the verbal, what you actually say, becomes 25 percent. Remember therefore that a simple word such as 'yes' can be said in a friendly tone inviting the caller to speak or it can also be shouted harshly, making the caller feel that you are too busy or too stressed to talk to them. Your tone therefore is all important to the success of that call.

Allow me to share with you a story told to me by Jade, one of my associates. It highlights what body language and vocal pitch and intonation means. This is her story.

> We were all at a hen do. That night there was
> a man coming in to run a workshop, teaching

us how to make cocktails. When he arrived, he was quiet and bumbling, he looked down constantly and introduced himself meekly as Nigel. He was reading out how to make cocktails from a shaking piece of paper and he was all-round awkward. He told us it was the first time he had hosted one of these parties. Naturally, everyone in the group was looking at each other, we all felt bad for him, but also uncomfortable. There is nothing worse than feeling sorry for someone who is supposed to be the presenter. A few minutes of unease later, he told us all that he was only joking. To our great relief, he immediately sprang into life as a charismatic and vivacious host and was like that for the rest of the evening. His name was really Nigel though.

What is apparent from Jade's story is that as long as someone appears awkward, mumbling with their eyes cast down and closed body language, no one is actually listening to what they are saying. We become nervous for them and are too distracted by the suppressed body language and painful hesitant speech. We stop listening to the words and just focus on the embarrassing situation.

There are notable individuals throughout history who realised the influence of body language for themselves and pioneered its uses long before any field of scientific study of it emerged. Some of the first known experts to consider body language were the Greeks and the Romans. Notable orators such as Socrates, Aristotle and Cicero began to understand specific dimensions of human physicality and employed these learnings in their own oration styles and teachings.

Later, in 1605, the English philosopher, politician and scientist, Francis Bacon, wrote the following in his work, *Of the proficience and advancement of learning, divine and human*, about what gestures tell us about someone:

> For Aristotle hath very ingeniously and diligently handled the factures of the body, but not the gestures of the body, which are no less comprehensible by art, and of greater use and advantage. For the lineaments of the body do disclose the disposition and inclination of the mind in general; but the motions of the countenance and parts do not only so, but do further disclose the present humour and state of the mind and will.

He also identified King James I of England as an expert in the art of body language: 'for as your majesty saith most aptly and elegantly, as the tongue speaketh to the ear, so the gesture speaketh to the eye'.

Looking at images of influential orators and leaders throughout history, whether political, spiritual or corporate, one striking commonality is the use of open body language. Think of images of Julius Caesar, Jesus Christ and Mahatma Ghandi. From all of these we instinctively recognise that an open stance equals confidence.

In pictures of King James I, you see him standing with arms outstretched away from the body in a sharing and collaborative stance. Such a stance, which also encourages the chest to open and the centre to lift, is what inspires confidence in the audience. They may not be able to verbalise it as open body language, they will be aware of it subliminally.

A modern version of open body language along with authenticity can be seen in Barack Obama, the former US president. What he shows is a continuous and relaxed way of speaking and moving: note how he walks, he remains centred with an open chest and when he speaks his pace is slow, considered and clear. You will rarely see him looking at a script or autocue. He is constantly looking out at the audience directly as if he's talking to them personally.

The introduction of silent film in the early 20th century created another group of body language experts: silent film actors. Without the use of audio or dialogue, these astute actors refined ways of expressing a character's thoughts, feelings and status through purely visual means. Charlie Chaplin is probably the most famous example of this art form.

Body language confidence

Body language and eye contact are essential to confident communication. However, confident, relaxed, open body language is not always easy to achieve, especially when we're nervous or out of touch with our own physicality.

Many physical techniques share the theory that the body's main energy emanates from the centre. This is the area around the belly button known as the solar plexus ('the sun' in Latin) or the chi in martial arts. Therefore, if energy emanates from this centre, it needs to be strong. In pilates and yoga, it is referred to as the core of the body, which needs to be kept lifted if posture is to look assertive and confident.

Exercises before you speak

Try these routines before you speak to help you feel better aligned and able to express yourself with composure and conviction.

- Stand with your feet a foot apart (about shoulder width). Knees relaxed. Stand tall.

- Breathe in, lifting rib cage. Keep shoulders down. Gently exhale breath. Imagine a thread from your belly button passing through your lower back and attached to a wall behind you.

- Shoulders should be relaxed and down at all times. To loosen, roll them backwards and forwards four times, really stretching them to a 360° circle. To check relaxation, lift and drop (tense and relax) your shoulders five or six times. Let them be as heavy as a sack of potatoes.

- Now imagine a string from the crown of your head to the ceiling lifting you up through your spinal column.

PHYSICAL COMMUNICATION

- Eyes focused on a point straight ahead, arms at your sides, centre lifted, weight evenly distributed between your feet, chin centrally positioned (beware of nose in the air or head tilted shyly down).

- Another deep breath through the nose and smile as you look out to your listeners (or energize your face by raising your eyebrows, if, like Gordon Brown, you are not a natural smiler).

Vocal exercises

Warm up your voice with humming:

- Find the comfortable middle note of your voice and move your mouth as if you have a hot potato in there. This helps to open your throat and all your speech organs. Try humming again. Touch your chest, cheeks, forehead and top of your head to feel the vibration of your resonance.

- Breathe deeply opening your rib cage and diaphragm without raising the shoulders and hum out to the count of ten with the first breath, hum to fifteen with the second breath and hum to twenty with the third breath.

- Rest for a few seconds, breathe in again and hum to five then open your mouth and ahhh to ten. Again hum to five and ahhh to fifteen, then finally breathe in and hum to five and ahhh to twenty. Make sure when you open your mouth, your jaw isn't locked, your tongue is relaxed on the floor of your mouth and that your throat feels open and free. As soon as you feel a constriction, stop, shake out, have a drink of water and try again.

When practicing your talk, ask a friend or colleague to feedback specifically on the vocal quality: intonation, pitch, pace, diction, pause and volume. If required, try to add some dynamism (light and shade) to your talk that will help make your message more expressive and engaging.

'People may hear your words, but they feel your attitude.'
John C Maxwell

5.
STORYTELLING

'Storytelling is the most powerful way to put ideas into the world today.'

Robert McAfee Brown

Since time immemorial, storytelling has been an integral part of human culture, binding communities together through oral traditions passed down from generation to generation. From Africa to Scandinavia and Fiji to Tibet, we share proverbs, fables, folk tales, poetry and song to transfer knowledge and wisdom, shape identity and communicate emotion. Think of the oratory epics from ancient Greece, Shakespeare's indelible plays of head and heart, Grimm's fairy tales and legends like those of Robin Hood and King Arthur. Stories are how we best understand both ourselves and the world around us.

Now let's take it one step further, make it a personal story. Personal stories make for riveting listening and powerful tools in presenting. Why? Because at one point or another, they give everyone in the audience a chance to relate to or link in with the story in their own way, to evoke a personal memory and see themselves within our world. This builds engagement, empathy and rapport.

I will tell you a story that I often share with clients when workshopping: it is of my first memory as a child. I remember being on the beach in Accra, Ghana, where my family was living at the time. On that West African coastline, the waves are huge with a forceful and dangerous undertow. I loved, and still do love, the sea and even at a very early age would throw myself into the huge surf without fear.

My first memory is of the strong undercurrent dragging me to the bottom of the seafloor. There, I walked on all fours, feeling the pull of the current above my head yet unable to force myself through it to reach for the surface. I remember thinking that if I didn't get to the surface I would drown, but I didn't mind. I felt I had enjoyed life (I was five), I loved the sea and it would be fine. I stayed there for what seemed like five minutes but was probably ten seconds. When the surf reversed and the waves started to come in again, the current ceased momentarily, and I popped to the surface.

STORYTELLING

Years later, when rational thought came into my consciousness, I wondered how it was that I hadn't drowned. Was it because I remained calm and didn't panic? Or could it be because I was born in a caul, an extra membrane found around the body of a newborn baby, like a sack, often around the head? In former times, sailors used to buy them, as the superstition held that they would never drown at sea if they had a caul. Thus, a baby born in a caul would never drown either.

When I tell this story to a group of people, each person will react in a different way to both the content and the visual pictures I produce. Quite often they will make connections with parts of their own childhood, such as being on the beach with their parents or the first time they swam. Others think about time they may have spent in Africa or the effect of not panicking in a crisis. Whatever it is that sparks the listener's memory or imagination is relevant because that is the start of engagement with an audience; each moment will be different and particular to the individual listener. By including stories, we can make the audience think about themselves. When what they hear somehow resonates with them, they become receptive to us.

PERSONAL PRESENCE

'If history were taught in the form of stories, it would never be forgotten.'

Rudyard Kipling

Personal stories are how we get to know each other and relate. In presenting we must use them to expose something of ourselves. Harness the incredible power of vulnerability in storytelling and you become infinitely more approachable. This silent connection builds the authenticity and trust that is so crucial in business.

Think of an anecdote that is the kind of story you may tell your friends in the pub on a Friday night. See how many of them somehow find a way to relate to it and tell you their similar story. For example, one person tells the story: 'you'll never guess what happened to me last week when I arrived at passport control, I discovered I had my son's passport instead of mine'.

Then once you have told the story, others will tell their passport stories, like the time they went swimming with their passport. From there, we often finish these stories with a short learning or value of what we will not do again or do better. 'Now I only keep my passport in the nightstand, so I always know where it is.'

Building from this premise, these personal stories

can be used in a work context. For example, Sophie tells the story of how she overcame the challenge of running a half marathon: the struggle of getting up each morning and training for a year in all weathers before eventually succeeding in crossing the finish line. From being someone who had never done sport in her life, she raised £2000 for a charity in mental health. Telling this story of her personal challenge and how she fought to train while working at her day job was a powerful and simple analogy of how in the same way, work problems or barriers can be overcome with planning, hard work and a motivation to support a good cause or wider purpose.

I shall never forget listening to Jude Kelly's story (who became artistic director of the Southbank Centre) about how she built the renowned West Yorkshire Playhouse in Leeds. As you can imagine, this large, iconic building took a huge amount of money and effort to create; it has three theatres, a restaurant, coffee and drinks bars, box office, costume store and stage-building workshop, as well as administrative offices for all the staff. As often happens with such major projects, they become subject to unforeseen costs, delays, obstacles and problems with stakeholders. Jude had run out of budget. One day, when even the contingency fund was gone and the contractor had refused to continue work unless monies were made available, she was on the verge of giving up.

Then she had an idea and decided she must have a conversation with the contractor. She found his address and arrived outside his house early one morning, waiting for him to come out for work. She stopped him and with all the passion she felt for what she was creating in that building, she extolled its virtues, explaining the opportunities it would give to the youth, to local culture, for jobs, for the arts and business in general, and even about how it would put Leeds on the map as a centre of modern theatre. The contractor listened. She shared with us, the listeners in the audience, that she had no children and explained to him, the contractor, that this project was her baby that she desperately wanted to live and thrive. She managed to persuade him to continue his work and he even lowered his price to make it happen.

This impassioned speech had motivated the contractor and as is often the case with such crises, once one challenge was resolved the rest began to fall into place. The project was completed to great acclaim.

What we see in this personal story is the persuasive power of passion and conviction. Belief in what you are doing gives others belief in what you are saying. Jude Kelly's determination, waiting for this man on his doorstep and expressing what the building meant to her and for the community changed his mind. People understand and empathise if they feel that sense of conviction.

When Jude told this story, the audience was composed of top-tier consultants and business corporations. They were silent and palpably touched; she received a standing ovation. They saw the relevance of telling a personal story to make a profound point. A point about human understanding and connection rather than just dryly running through the technical and financial details of how the Yorkshire Playhouse was constructed. It was powerful, wholehearted, full of vulnerability and heartwarming.

A final example of personal storytelling comes from Ed Miliband speaking at the 2011 Labour Party Conference when he opened by saying:

> There's one person I want to thank more than any other.
> For her love, her support, for her encouragement.
> My wife Justine.
> Ask me the three most rewarding things I've done this year.
> Being at the birth of our second son Sam. Then

getting married. It is 2011 after all. And starting to tell Daniel, my older son, the stories my dad used to tell me.

Don't get hung up on thinking a story always has to be in a traditional format of a neat beginning, middle and end. What is important is the honest sharing of ourselves. When Ed Miliband revealed these simple personal truths, he showed his humanity and boosted his popularity by being more relatable.

Storytelling tips

So what makes a good story? Here are some elements of a good story you can use when crafting your presentations.

- Use people's names. For example, saying 'my sister Laura' instead of just 'my sister' makes it feel more personal.

- Keep any single story to under three minutes. It should enhance and support your main subject, not dilute or overshadow it.

STORYTELLING

- It must be a true story. Citing other people's stories is fine if done transparently, as is some embellishment, but never fabricate false stories. Your audience can tell and will perceive you as inauthentic and untrustworthy. If you're really struggling for a story, then dig into history. It's likely to be littered with examples of what you're trying to convey.

- Have a reveal. A good story needs to build to something, however minor it should include something of interest we didn't fully see coming.

- Humour is absolutely wonderful and recommended to create a light tone. Just don't use set jokes. Keep it natural.

- Get creative and find the link to what you're talking about. Introduce characters and conflict to help bring your facts and figures alive.

- What does your story reveal about you? Consider the characteristics that your story suggests about you and make sure that these are suitable for the context you are speaking in.

PERSONAL PRESENCE

- Emphasise any difficult words for the audience with repetition.

- Stories are often emotionally charged. See the chapter on structure to understand the importance of practising them aloud before sharing them.

- Try to remember some moments in your life that are emblazoned on your memory and for whatever reason are significant. Write them down. Try telling them out loud.

- Remember: any story is a good story.

6.
ENGAGING YOUR AUDIENCE

'In order to understand another person's point of view, you have to climb inside their shoes and walk around in them.'
Atticus Finch in Harper Lee's *To Kill a Mockingbird*

We have gone through how to recognise our strengths and overcome our fears, using physical and vocal exercises to allay our anxiety and nerves. We can term the three foundations always required to engage as:

- Knowing our strengths
- Body language and vocal tone
- Storytelling

Now let's go deeper into the texture of what the audience wants. When it comes to engagement, it's all about our audience. We need to understand who it is we're speaking to. Giving a talk about mountaineering, for example, will be different when given to a group of school leavers than to senior citizens. Correct pitching is of paramount importance. Whether your audience comprises five or 500 people, before you prepare to speak, ask yourself these questions:

- Who is my audience?
- What does this audience need from me?
- What do they want to hear?
- How can I convey my message in a way that will be relevant to them?

I once gave a lecture on presentation skills to 70 students taking an MBA course at the University of Lancaster. There were 25 different nationalities in the room and I had the weighty task of keeping them all engaged for four hours. How did I achieve this?

The first thing was big energy. In a large room, presence is key. Occupy the stage with your body, move across the whole space, keeping your body language open and projecting your voice. Use gestures and include visual pictures to create dynamism.

The next thing is eye contact: scan the room and make an effort to catch the gaze of every audience member individually throughout your talk. When possible, I also make an effort to try to learn and use individuals' names. If the set-up of the day will allow you, arrive early and meet people as they come in. Shake their hands, look them in the eye and say their names aloud twice as you greet them, which will help you commit them to memory. Then refer to them personally whenever possible as you interact later on.

Beginning with a rhetorical question is a strong opener as it immediately gets the audience thinking and therefore engaged. To be clear, a rhetorical question is one that you pose as the speaker and you also answer. The technique is to pause between the question and the answer, so the listeners have time to digest the question. For example, 'how do companies gauge their success?'. You, as the presenter, then answer your own question following the pause.

Later on, I ask non-rhetorical questions and repeat them three times so the students are comfortable to answer out loud. It is important to sense the audience and react. If you notice some of them glazing over or fidgeting, then respond and try to mix it up; introduce some more energy, change pace, ask a question or tell a story.

One key part of public speaking that's often overlooked is listening. I know it doesn't always feel this way, but a presentation should actually be a two-way communication, a living moment with information passing back and forth between speaker and audience. Listening to your audience, no matter how big or small, is essential. By paying attention and watching people's body language, eye contact and facial expressions, we can tell whether they are engaged with us and if our message is being well received. A skilled presenter will always read the room and adjust course as necessary. In the same way an actor in performance listens to how much coughing or fidgeting there is in the auditorium; when a thousand people fidget it is loud and when a thousand people smile you can hear them.

So, what else can we do to encourage engagement from our audience? One of the fundamentals is to build empathy with them by creating connections between you and the audience. Make yourself relatable, approachable and human. You could achieve this by referring directly to the audience, remembering the names of individuals or companies as we've mentioned. If you won't know anyone there personally, then research them ahead of time to get a sense of who they are (either individually or as a demographic if a big group) and think about the tone and touchpoints that will resonate with them.

Another great way is by pinpointing and referencing experiences they will recognise. For example, if you were talking about a disruptive change within the company, you could use an analogy of a time of change in your own personal life, such as moving to a new house or becoming a parent. Unless you're addressing the under 20s, then these are two fairly universal and relatable life events so would be a safe bet for making a connection between you and the audience, helping to give your message of company change some emotional charge for them. Remember the power of personal storytelling.

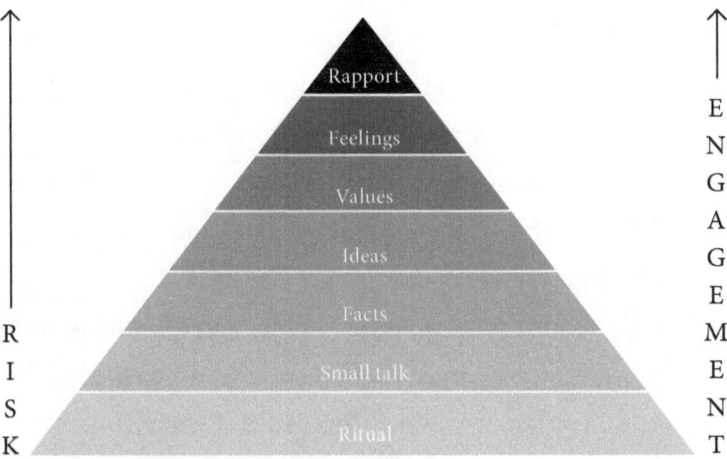

Figure 6.1: levels of communication

When we first meet someone, particularly in a business context, we greet them with rituals, such as shaking hands and asking after their general welfare. These are the rituals we all understand. We are likely to then move into cliché and familiar small talk, mentioning the weather or which route we took to get to the meeting; innocuous exchanges to cover the possible awkwardness of the first meeting. We may then progress to the facts at hand, details of the meeting, such as what are we here to achieve, what the project is about, what tasks shall we undertake and so on. Quite often this is as far as we go in a corporate setting because if we climb much further up the communication triangle we put ourselves at risk that our ideas and opinions will be mocked, rejected or challenged. So in many corporate settings, we thwart the chance of any real engagement process happening, because we fail to explore the more human dimensions of communication, those which pose a risk to us. Heaven forbid that we should then exchange ideas and even feelings. But with greater risk, comes far greater reward.

'I feel that this project needs an injection of collaborative thinking'; or 'my feelings are that we need to challenge the whole premise'; or even more disclosure, 'I am feeling rather low about this programme'.

What we miss by not communicating our ideas and feelings is that peak point of rapport, when we know we have made a mutual connection, built trust and can now work honestly, comfortably and collaboratively.

It is exactly the same whether we speak one to one, in a group or to a large audience. We need to present our true ideas and feelings so as to ultimately build rapport with that group or audience.

Even if you're presenting in a formal or corporate setting, don't be afraid to show some of your natural warmth and personality. After all, however stern that boss or client may sometimes seem, we're all only human. Smiling, humility, honesty and humour work wonders. Try not to take yourself too seriously. The more relaxed you are, the more relaxed the audience will be, and this inevitably endears them towards you.

Though I often recommend a healthy sprinkling of humour in public speaking, use good judgement as to what it should look like in any given context. Steer clear of contrived jokes and gags, and keep content apolitical. I've been at engagements and seen skilful speakers lose favour with half the room in one fell swoop by sharing a distasteful joke. A work presentation probably isn't the best time to try out your stand-up routine.

In a conference situation if you have the opportunity to make reference to something relevant that an earlier speaker said, it shows you are an active listener and makes them feel acknowledged. It also creates a welcome link between talks for the audience.

A quick side note about hecklers. Let's say we're at the same conference and we get a heckler, don't panic, I'm not suggesting you'll ever have an obnoxious drunk booing you off stage or hurling peanuts at your head during your talk on data systems. But in the unlikely event of an interruption, simply remain polite and positive: 'good question, I'll come back to it at the end' or 'I'll be coming to it in my presentation'.

If it's a repeat question, then smilingly: 'no problem, as I mentioned earlier…'; as opposed to, 'I've already answered that, someone's clearly not paying attention'.

Whilst it can certainly be irksome to have your flow and train of thought disrupted, remember no one is deliberately trying to sabotage you. They are simply keen on seeking clarification on something. Remain calm. If we become irritated or display temper, we lose gravitas, whereas keeping one's composure shows we are in control. Our words gain credence and we keep the audience focused, rather than distracted by sensing we are in a flap.

PowerPoint

Ok, we've talked about what makes an engaging presentation. But what can make a presentation disengaging? Well, apart from doing the opposite of all the advice given above, PowerPoint.

A common answer I hear when asked, 'how's your

presentation coming on?' is something like, 'well, I've got 30 slides'. A PowerPoint display does not a presentation make. Yet it has somehow become synonymous in organizations that PowerPoint equals presentation. Some people feel so strongly about this overuse of presentation software that they have formed the Anti-PowerPoint Party of Switzerland, a group of international citizens 'dedicated to decreasing professional use of PowerPoint and other presentation software', which they claim, 'causes national economic damage amounting to 2.1 billion Swiss francs' and lowers the quality of a presentation in 95 percent of cases. Whilst my feelings on it aren't quite strong enough to begin rabble-rousing in parliament, I do agree that it is poorly and painfully overused in most instances.

PowerPoint (if used at all) should enhance what we are saying and not distract. Pictures, charts and graphs can often be helpful in getting a message across more visually, but don't be tempted to include too much information: start clean and simple, and build if necessary. As a rule of thumb, no more than five slides in five minutes.

A keyword or title can bring emphasis to a point you are making, but it is a common mistake to create slides with dense lists, bullet points or full sentences. These will only encourage the audience to begin reading and thinking about what you might say, rather than listening attentively to what you are actually saying. Remember that they are there to hear you. Lazy presentation is lots of text slides, so the audience is left reading. In these instances, most of us would probably rather go home to read it rather than sitting in an auditorium.

Something else I see a lot are bullet points written up on PowerPoint as a sort of safety net for the presenter. Tempting as it may seem, steer clear of relying on PowerPoint as your memory aid; this is certainly a job for cue cards (which I will speak more about later in the chapter on structure). It's important that you know your presentation and PowerPoint by heart. Looking at your audience and making eye contact whilst you explain any slides will win you their attention and engagement. If you keep needing to look back at your PowerPoint for cues, it is no longer possible; the audience will lose eye contact with you and break any connection that you've built with them up to that point. It can be easy to lose an audience's attention completely in this way. By facing forward and maintaining visual contact, you'll also be able to read in their faces whether they are receiving what you are saying. If they are not, then don't be afraid to repeat it.

If you need to talk about technical data and statistics, it is strongly recommended to include no more than three data points in a short presentation of up to five minutes.

Anymore and the audience simply won't retain them. More detailed information can always be circulated after the talk for people to refer to and digest at their own convenience (print-outs, memory sticks, mailshots etc).

It's also worth noting that sometimes the more friendly flip chart (championed by the Anti-PowerPoint Party) is more suitable than a slide. It is tactile, in the room and works especially well for more intimate situations with the added bonus of removing any technical worries, which is great if you are already nervous and not particularly tech savvy, or just can't be sure what the venue's audiovisual set-up will be. Consider whether this trusty option could, in fact, meet your needs instead.

We all prefer to listen to people than suffer death by PowerPoint. The human voice, body, gestures, presence and real contact are what people spark off. That is how your message will be remembered. You are more interesting than a PowerPoint any day or time.

Team presentations

Presenting in a team is different in many ways to doing it alone. There's a reason you are speaking as a team rather than individually, so it is important that this comes across; that a team dynamic is palpable. These are not multiple solo pitches running parallel but rather all about collaboration and showcasing to your audience how well you complement, understand and support each other. Here are some useful reminders when pitching or presenting with others.

First up, use each other's names both when introducing and throughout. It shows familiarity and helps build these links with the audience.

When you introduce a colleague, make eye contact with them and use an open palm hand gesture. This tells us that you empower your team and see them as your equals, and the silent connection suggests that you're engaged with them collaboratively. Failing to look at your fellow team members, and acknowledging only the audience, disregards them and suggests ego. This doesn't give the audience faith that you have a conducive team dynamic, essential to any successful business.

Actively listen to your team-mates as they speak; no reading what you are about to say or staring at your shoes. Whilst they are talking, listen and look at them, then out to the audience. This eye movement helps take your colleague's message out to the listener and again makes the all-important silent connection. It shows co-operation and that you all work well together, not just solo.

Make a concerted effort to make eye contact with everyone in the room, not only who you believe is the decision-maker. Everyone is as important as each other. I have seen important bids being presented by a team of four people. The members of the team as they speak look mainly at the chief executive or the financial director as the person they assume is the decision-maker and ignore the other people on the panel. That is not the way to win clients and influence people, as you are excluding all those other decision-makers.

Typically, at the end of a team pitch, there will be time for questions and answers. Think through and discuss ahead of time what questions you may all be asked. Doing a dry run and practising some role-play questions with each other will help prepare you and build trust between you. One person should take the lead on fielding questions and be prepared with answers for all of them if necessary, but each member of the team should answer at least one question. You are a team and not just support to the lead.

Get to know each other's body language to read who feels comfortable answering each question. We want to avoid dropping each other in it and saying, 'oh, my colleague will answer that', if you're not sure that they can. Let's look out for each other. And if you personally don't know the answer, then don't pretend to. Waffling on or blagging it looks incompetent and insincere. People respect those who are honest as it builds trust. Much better to say: 'sorry, I don't have the answer to that right now, but I'll check with x' or 'I'll find out and come back to you by close of play today'. Being specific with a timeframe goes down well as it shows you aren't just fobbing them off and genuinely care about finding out for them.

Engagement exercises

- Practise your active listening by not speaking in a group meeting for ten minutes.

- Use people's names and refer to them.

- Try delivering your next talk without PowerPoint.

- Practise introducing two colleagues who are either side of you: make sure that you make eye contact and gesture toward them when you say their names.

7.
LESSONS FROM THE GREEKS: RULE OF THREE

'Truth, simplicity and sincerity are most congenial to man's nature.'

Cicero

The significance of the number three underlies much of human history. The Pythagoreans taught that the number three was the first true number: it is the first number that forms a geometrical figure, the triangle. It is considered a number of good fortune, third time lucky, and as the number of harmony, wisdom and understanding. Three is also the number of time: past, present and future; birth, life and death; beginning, middle and end.

As a sacred number in many religions, we perhaps know it most commonly here in the West in the context of Christianity with three representing the holy trinity of the father, the son and the holy ghost. Or mind, body and spirit. All three must be in balance to be centred and wholly human.

This divine number is seen prolifically throughout Greek mythology and the ancient Greeks understood its power in oration. The Greeks described oration in terms of pathos (emotion), ethos (values) and logos (logic).

Pathos is that which appeals to the audience's emotions, values and interests. Ethos is our credibility, authenticity and values as the orator. Logos speaks to the logic and reasoning of the argument with reference to facts and statistics of context.

In Aristotle's rhetorical triangle, he surmised that in order to put forth any sound and compelling argument, we need to incorporate all three into our writing and presentation. Rhetoric (from the Greek *rhētorike tekhnē*, the art of an orator) is the ancient art of using language to persuade; when we use all three of ethos, pathos and logos in our public speaking, we become highly persuasive to our audience:

- **Pathos, emotion and the audience**: emotional or imaginative impact; stories; experiential proof; relatable anecdotes; inspirational quotes; vivid language; connection; 'I feel …'.

LESSONS FROM THE GREEKS: RULE OF THREE

- **Ethos, credibility and you the speaker**: trustworthiness; reputation; personal branding; confidence in delivery; citing credible sources; tone and style; body language; values; leadership; personal integrity.

- **Logos, logic and the context**: reasoning; facts, figures, data and case studies; clearly structured argument; analogies and metaphors.

Whilst all three of these aspects play an important part in constructing a persuasive argument, they are not all equally weighted. It's worth taking a moment to acknowledge a well-established, and perhaps uncomfortable, truth about human nature. Although we often like to think of ourselves as rational beings, it is in fact emotion (pathos) that holds the greatest sway over many of our decisions and behaviours. Emotion, not reason or credibility, has the power to compel us one way or another. Sound familiar? It might be sending a 4.00 am text message, adopting that too cute third pet, booking the unaffordable plane ticket, or championing one football team over another. The influence of our emotions can be observed in every corner of our lives.

In his book, *The Happiness Hypothesis*, acclaimed psychologist and researcher Jonathan Haidt depicts a useful metaphor to illustrate the conflict we all have between our rational and emotional selves. He characterizes our emotional side as an elephant and our rational mind as the elephant's rider. Sitting atop the elephant, the rational rider feels in control of steering which way they go. However, if there is a disagreement in which path to take, it will be the elephant, far greater in size and power than the rider, who will determine their course.

Knowing the integral role that emotions play in forming our opinions and behaviours, think of ways you can inject some more emotion into your presentation in order to compel and have a lasting impact on your audience. Stories are more memorable and galvanising to us than just facts or statistics as they appeal to our emotions, which are the key to unlocking engagement and building rapport when speaking.

Three-card oratory trick

Just as we have a three-card trick in games like poker and brag, I call the technique of using three words or phrases together to express one idea the three-card oratory trick. It follows from the rhetorical technique traced back to ancient Greece known as the rule of three. This principle suggests that there is something inherently more satisfying

LESSONS FROM THE GREEKS: RULE OF THREE

or effective to the human ear in hearing things in threes than in other numbers. It is just enough information to give credibility and rhythm, but not so much that it cannot be retained in our limited short-term memory.

The rule of three is a technique used the world over for centuries and once you start looking you'll be able to spot countless examples. Perhaps one of the most well-known and influential is from the US Declaration of Independence penned by Thomas Jefferson; 'life, liberty, and the pursuit of happiness'. Which subsequently inspired the French motto: 'liberty, equality, fraternity'.

You may remember Tony Blair saying, 'education, education, education'. To which the response from Sir Richard Eyre, director of the National Theatre, was, 'disappointment, disappointment, disappointment'.

Even as children, threes are everywhere. The three musketeers. Three little pigs. Flopsy, Mopsy and Cottontail. Here are some examples of the rule of three used wonderfully:

- 'I'm not talking about the budget deficit. I'm not talking about the trade deficit. I'm talking about the moral deficit in this country', Barack Obama.

- 'Veni, vidi, vici' ('I came, I saw, I conquered'), Julius Caesar.

- 'A rock, A river, A tree.', Maya Angelou from *On the Pulse of the Morning.*

Exercises in three

Try using the rule of three in different ways in your next presentation.

- Present just three key findings, selling points or benefits.

- Craft three stories to convey your message.

- Use the three-card oratory trick to group key ideas into trios of words or phrases. Triplets of adjectives work wonders when describing important concepts or characters, eg, he was witty, bright and inspiring.

- If you want people in the audience to answer a question you pose, then ask it three times in slightly different ways. This repetition of three, not unlike pantomime characters asking kids for help, creates buy-in from the audience and makes them comfortable enough to participate.

8.
STRUCTURE

Structure is the hook to hang your coat on. It is also one of the things I get asked for most by clients wishing to improve their presentation skills. People like to have something concrete, a framework they can build around, especially any of us who are more analytically minded.

Proper structure can and should be used for any type of presentation, be it a business pitch, eulogy, wedding speech or team talk. I once got a call out of the blue in the early hours. It was from an executive guy I hadn't worked with before but was seeking my help having just delivered a presentation. It had gone terribly. He said he'd somehow just fallen apart up there. He seemed genuinely dumbfounded explaining:

'But I'm really good at presenting.'

'Did you prepare?', I asked.

'I never prepare.'

Mystery solved. We all need to have some structure and method of preparation when we're planning to give a talk. Even if you feel extremely confident on the subject matter and are naturally gifted at public speaking, we're all human and things can throw us. Don't be complacent.

To give yourself not just peace of mind, but the best chance of knocking it out of the park, take some time to lay the groundwork for your presentation. It really will work wonders for your skills as you become increasingly comfortable with the format of a well-structured talk.

Let's look at the five salient points of presentation, a practical format to help you construct your talk.

Impact opening

Always start your presentation with a bang. This attention grabber will engage your audience from the outset and make them want more. We all know the worst presentations start with: 'Um, I thought I'd, er, tell you, um, about my, er, work. My name is, er', etc.

You could use a relevant quote, strong statement or a rhetorical question. I know a lot of people who are nervous when they start speaking, but if you have a strong opening line that you know off by heart, it will reduce this unease and make you feel far more comfortable:

STRUCTURE

- 'Last year our company lost £2 billion.'

- 'The best moment of my life was watching my son being born.'

- 'When was the last time you knew you were in exactly the right place at the right time?'

Comments like these will certainly capture people's attention and get them listening.

Refer to your audience

When possible (not practical when addressing large audiences), use the names of people you are speaking to. Refer to occasions when you have worked closely together. For example: 'remember when we all stayed up until 11:00 pm working on that project for x? Wasn't that a valuable collaborative experience?'.

Making a direct connection with the listener makes them feel acknowledged and it can relax the dynamic in the room making for a more conversational tone. If you don't know anyone personally, then try to do some research on them or their company to get a sense of who they are and what they may want to hear. Use collaborative language (we, us, our).

Pose questions to give them food for thought and get them participating mentally. These can be rhetorical:

- 'Wouldn't it be great if we managed to achieve our goals for this year?'.

- 'I am sure you are all aware …'

Three key messages

We're back to the rule of three. Three is proven to be an optimal number, as it is the amount most people can easily remember. If you don't have three key messages, then less is absolutely fine, but avoid the temptation to go for five or six, as you risk your audience remembering nothing.

It may be three key values, three findings or even storytelling with past, present and future. For example, what can your company offer their clients? Trust, approachability and technical expertise. Then you can give examples around these three messages.

I also advise splitting your presentation into three chunks: opening, body and conclusion. A good approach can be to briefly summarise the three key messages early on, so people know what you're going to cover. Then signpost back to them again in your closing section to help them stick in the audience's mind. Repetition is your friend. Repetition is your friend.

Analogy, anecdote and example

With every hard fact or statement you make, I recommend having a real-world example or analogy to make it clear and relatable. Every anecdote not only illuminates the point but also engages the listener. Ideally try to come up with an analogy, story or real-world example to support or illustrate each of your three key messages. This is where storytelling can come to the fore.

Succinct last line

Just as we started strong, let's make sure we finish strong too. Close your talk with a concrete last line and firm enunciation on every word. Just like 'happily ever after' in a children's story. For example: '... and that is why I believe wholeheartedly (pause) in education for all'.

It should be clear from the intonation pattern of the speaker's voice that we have reached the end and usually it is the last four words that we emphasize.

Most people peter out with a rather flat: '... and I think that's all I have to say ... yes ... I don't think there's anything else, okay, thanks'. Which is pretty uninspiring. Instead, like the impact opener, you can close with a clear, concise statement, a quote or even a question.

Let's imagine you have your clearly structured and content-rich talk all drafted. It's peppered with threes and packed with personal storytelling. Great job. It's now time for an all-important step: practice, practice, practice.

Practice

Practice is one of the best ways to gain confidence and see noticeable improvements in your public speaking. The more times you can run through your talk out loud, the better. Three times is a minimum. No need to read it word for word; much better, in fact, use prompts (cue cards) so that each time it will be delivered slightly differently and remain fresh and sincere sounding, not robotically recited.

Actors and musicians drill their pieces until they become part of their organic being. At that point, it becomes so embedded that it can then be played around with in a more natural, confident and expressive way. So, practice in front of the mirror, practice in the shower or whilst walking the dog, practice to your partner, friends or colleagues, practice in the car or doing the hoovering. You get the idea.

Remember to time yourself a couple of times to make

sure it's an appropriate length. Hearing ourselves aloud is different to reading in our heads and as you hear yourself you will also be able to get a clearer sense of how it will come across to your audience. If you have a new idea or something isn't quite working, like a phrase is tripping you up, then feel free to change it. This is your presentation, so you can shape and evolve it as you see fit. If you can work on it far enough ahead of time, without being under the cosh, then this iterative and creative process can even be fun. (Shocking I know.) Enjoy it and be proud knowing that you are giving it your attention. No one can ask for more than your best, even you, and doing this thorough prep work will give you that feeling of satisfaction and readiness on the day to relax and deliver your best.

In group workshops, I ask participants to each bring a story to share with the group. It can be anything, they just have to tell it out loud. One day I was working with a group of five and it came to Ian's turn to speak. He told us a story of when he had been working as a consultant for the rail industry in the early 2000s. It was during a difficult period when there had been a high number of serious rail accidents in the United Kingdom. On Ian's first day, he was sent to a meeting for the rail victims and families involved in the Ladbroke Grove disaster in 1999, a tragic event which killed 31 people and injured 238 on the Great Western Line. There,

Ian spoke with a man who had lost his 18-year-old son. He had told Ian how, to help get over the death of his son, he had meticulously constructed a complete, to-scale model reproduction of the Ladbroke Grove station in his attic. At this point of telling the story, Ian faltered and we saw he had tears running down his cheeks. He had to stop speaking and I encouraged him to breathe and take his time. The group was mesmerized.

'Have you ever told this story before?', I asked. He hadn't, not even to his wife. He was saying it out loud for the first time and the unexorcized emotion of the memory proved too raw, taking hold of his physiology. Once we verbalize our stories, they become real, often for the first time. Stories hold emotion and emotion has power. This is an example of why it is essential to say your talk out loud at least three times before presenting. That way the emotion of what you're saying, which is so valuable, will remain authentic but without catching you off guard and becoming physically overwhelming. Practice out loud and you will maintain control of your emotions and body.

An exercise in structure

- Think firstly of your three key messages.

STRUCTURE

- What are the stories or analogies that match those messages?

- Create your impact opening and punchy last line.

- Think of your audience and what they need and want to hear.

9.
SELF-DISCLOSURE, SELF-AWARENESS, SELF-CONFIDENCE

'When people talk, listen completely. Most people never listen.'

Ernest Hemmingway

When I was in my early 20s, my then boyfriend once told me that when he'd first met me, he thought I came across as a cold, posh bitch. Charming, I know. Though perhaps not the kindest of phrasing, I acknowledged his comments without offence. With some reflection, I noted that due to my tallness (I'm 5' 11"), it could seem that I looked down my nose at people. I'd also unwittingly developed a tendency for sticking my nose in the air in defiance of my two brothers whilst growing up, which gave me a slightly haughty air. It

SELF-AWARENESS, SELF-DISCLOSURE, SELF-CONFIDENCE

didn't help my case that I also rarely smiled at that time; it was 1971 and in those days it was often perceived as a come-on from a woman to be too friendly. I decided to consciously work on bringing my chin down and I began smiling more. I actually discovered that I'm a natural smiler and had just been holding back. This did indeed have the desired effect of making me much more approachable.

How we see ourselves is important, but equally so is having an honest understanding of how others see us. They are two sides of the same coin, two complementing forms of self-awareness, and we need to integrate them both to become the best communicators we can be. Being confident in who you are is a wonderful thing but to be an effective leader, motivator or public speaker, you also need to have a heightened awareness of how you come over, not just self-confidence, but awareness of the effect you have on others, how you make them feel. An example of the difference between self-confidence and self-awareness are politicians who have led elite and sheltered lives. They can be hugely self-confident yet unaware of how they come across to the public, especially to people from different walks of life. Too much self-confidence, without the tempering of self-awareness, can even become delusion.

One notably poor presentation I saw was actually from a trained actor who was pitching in a professional environment. He did the whole thing in the style of a pantomime dame and, although he gave a funny and confident performance, it was just that, a performance, and not a presentation. By wearing the mask of a character, he was inauthentic, and the audience struggled to really know who he was and therefore build the trust required to want to do business with him.

For some people, self-awareness and perceptiveness in social interactions come naturally, while others are less intuitive. Think of a person you know who you think comes across well in a range of situations, someone you feel embodies a strong sense of self-awareness. Now think of somebody you know who you feel is more towards the other end of the self-awareness spectrum. Perhaps they appear fairly confident, but they tend to say and do things that are not always well received, they seem dulled (or oblivious) to how their words and actions make others feel. Now consider honestly which qualities you share with each of these two people. Is there any crossover or similarity? Where on this continuum of self-awareness do you think you might be at the moment? Whichever spot it is, happily, self-awareness is a muscle we all have the ability to strengthen with some practice. The key is to be mindful.

The Johari Window, a classic psychological tool developed by Jo Luft and Harry Ingham in the 1950s, shows how feedback and self-disclosure act to build our self-awareness.

SELF-AWARENESS, SELF-DISCLOSURE, SELF-CONFIDENCE

Figure 9.1: The Johari Window

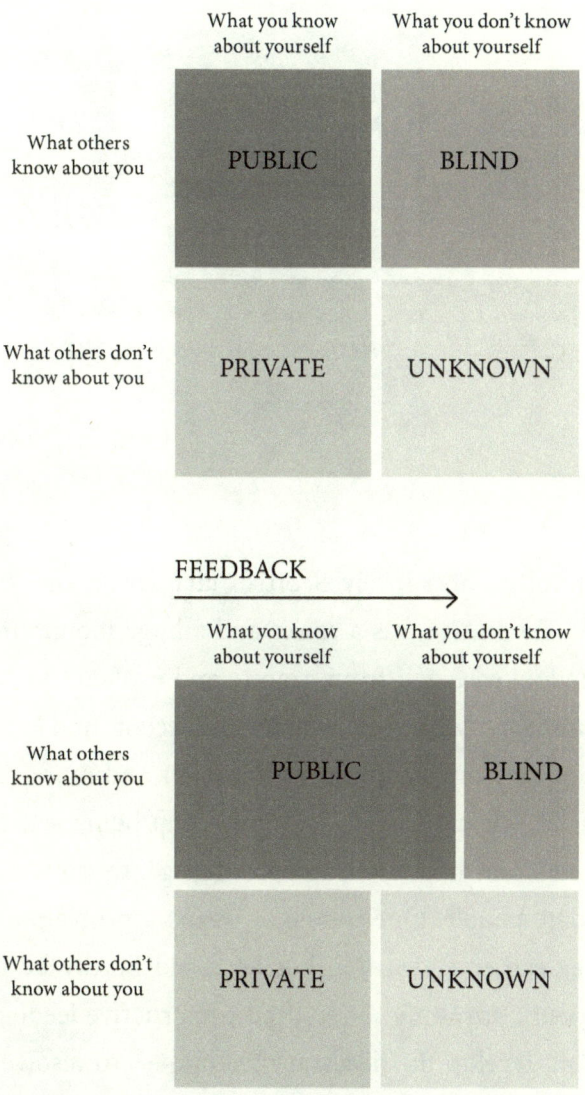

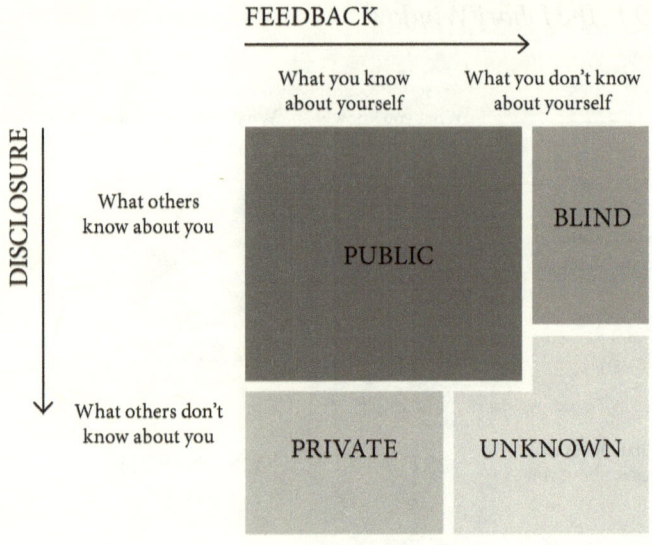

I'm reminded of a lovely Scottish chap from one of my courses, Gavin. He was a rower and a huge mountain of a guy. He looked hewn from granite and evoked the battles of *Braveheart* with his wonderful accent and rugged, imposing physicality, but he spoke softer and more quietly than a church mouse. He had grown up being self-aware of his size and had taken to speaking gently so as not to intimidate people. One to one, it wasn't a problem and in fact was rather endearing, but he could hardly be heard when public speaking so required constructive feedback to help him develop the necessary techniques to resolve this.

SELF-AWARENESS, SELF-DISCLOSURE, SELF-CONFIDENCE

Feedback is important to help us balance out our view of ourselves.

If self-awareness and self-disclosure are key to positive communication, we need to understand ourselves well. Therefore, being truthful and sincere allows us to be open; the more open we are with our audience, the more we disclose, the more we disclose the more people understand us and can relate to our ideas and feelings. This feedback loop of emotional intelligence (EI) provides powerful growth.

The more you self-disclose, for example, through storytelling, the more the public arena of you and your values are shared with the audience. This is a chance to make yourself relatable and again make that silent connection. Use your own good judgement of which story to share. Disclosure exists in the context of vulnerability and humility; it does not mean oversharing. Pouring out the gnarly details of our divorce on social media is not healthy disclosure.

By purposefully listening to feedback and putting focus and attention into seeing, hearing and feeling how others react to us, however subtly, we can all increase our levels of self-awareness and enjoy the benefits of this invaluable life and business skill.

The unknown in the Johari window is our potential,

or the learning we still have ahead of us, to discover as we age. We each progress along this path of self-learning and personal excavation until the day we die. We may as well work to be conscious and purposeful as we walk it, enjoying the insights as they unfold.

Exercises in feedback and disclosure

Your thumbnail sketch

With a trusted (but impartial) partner, work out how the world sees you in just three or four adjectives. What is the generalized, thumbnail sketch of you to others? It may include a physical characteristic. It may even include a slightly negative word, it is all useful and can serve as a cause for reflection. For example: tall, reliable, generous, bossy.

Practise disclosure

Include a short personal story whenever you are next presenting or even just talking in a group. Anything true to you that you haven't shared before. Take a risk and disclose perhaps something you are not so proud of in yourself. See the reaction within a small group and then try it in a larger group. The undeniable build of empathy and rapport will be palpable. People will see you are human and will begin to trust you.

Feedback

Ask for feedback and try it in a group of three, one giving the feedback, one receiving and the other observing. The observer can comment on how the feedback was delivered, how it was received and how it came over to them as an impartial witness. Then change places and watch how others do the job you have just done.

10.
ELEVATOR PITCHES AND SPEAKING TO CAMERA

How many of you have had the experience of an elevator pitch? You have a minute to deliver your most important messages or thoughts to the person you wish to inspire before the lift door opens on the next floor. It may be a chief executive, if you are in management; or an investor, if you're a new venture. You need to be succinct, friendly, well paced and make an impact. Quite a task.

In the same way, if you are a chief executive and you are in the lift with a junior recruit, it is your responsibility to make that person feel engaged and noticed. Most senior executives are so busy, they don't have time to talk to new intakes.

Yet as we all know, if you give your focus, attention and time to the young, they will be inspired to work harder and summon their creativity. Ultimately, as they grow, your company will grow. It seems simple but is not often practiced in reality.

Let's prepare. Think of three key messages that you think are important to you, your work and your life. Make them short and succinct. Add a story to back up your beliefs and practice out loud. Next time you are at a networking event or in a meeting, have your messages ready to deliver. Obviously, you will need to make modifications, depending on your audience.

And when you meet a new or younger member of staff, ask questions of them and listen to what they say. Now it's about them and not you. Listening is all important. You may find they want to know your values or something about your work, then you have the opportunity to share. In theatre, we say 'acting is re-acting'. In the same way you are reacting to something given to you, rather than delivering yourself in a vacuum. Think of your audience.

Doorstep challenges

An even more testing situation is the exercise known as 'the doorstep challenge', which I experienced as a facilitator in the United States. A group of senior executives is sitting at table eating breakfast at 6.30 am awaiting a programme day on executive presence. They are called individually away from their seats by a facilitator, taken outside the restaurant and shown a placard on which is written: 'why should anyone be led by you?'.

They then see a camera and microphone and in one minute they have to make a persuasive argument for their role as a leader. I am sure you can imagine that, unprepared, many of them stuttered, panicked, gabbled their words, took shallow breaths or were completely tongue tied, looking most unlike leaders. A few however understood that with warmth, eye contact, a moderate pace and open body language, you are halfway there.

The same premise applies as when you are practising your elevator pitch. You have three key messages up your sleeve for all these occasions: what you believe in, who you are and what's important, for example. It's up to you, of course, which messages best give a sense of the authentic you.

Speaking to camera

When I was giving masters' programmes in project management and leadership for NHS executives, I remember that it was common for these unfortunate souls to be met by a large fluffy microphone as they stepped out of the back door of the hospital where they worked. They used

ELEVATOR PITCHES AND SPEAKING TO CAMERA

the back door in the hope that they weren't doorstepped by the media. All too often that didn't work. The large fluffy mic was shoved under their noses with extremely direct and difficult questions like:

- 'Why are so many people lying on trollies in the corridors, especially the elderly, including my wife's uncle?'

- or 'Why is it that many British people are having to go to Poland to have hip replacements?'

Of course, there are answers to these types of question, but you need to be ready and relaxed to answer with confidence and authority. Breathing exercises are essential. Always take a deep breath before replying. It gives you time to think and shows that you are in the moment, thinking the answer through carefully. The media holds no prisoners.

The next challenge is, of course, speaking to camera. Much the same applies as above. However physical centring, relaxation and direct eye contact will immediately grab the audiences' attention. If you are speaking directly to camera as one alone, then you need to look into the lens and imagine it's your favourite person, your partner, husband or wife, mother, father or child, or even best friend, whoever is the person you feel most comfortable with. Imagine that you are speaking to your audience as if they were sitting in your own living room. In this way, you will talk conversationally and with some warmth which will give you the gravitas you desire. You are talking to another person, not a camera. Practice in front of a mirror before being filmed. Take note of your own physical mannerisms both on your face and your whole body. Ask yourself how you are coming across. This is a continuation of your self-awareness journey. Don't be afraid to ask the camera person how much of you is 'in frame', whether it's a close-up of just your face or a long shot of your whole body.

When in a TV studio, as well as making eye contact with your interviewer, make sure that you also turn your body and your gaze towards the front to the camera that has a red light on and towards the audience. It can be difficult as your focus is in two places at least. But if you just look at the interviewer and you have a studio audience, it will appear that you are not sharing your ideas and thoughts and you aren't interested in them. Sharing requires open-body and open-arm gestures.

When using autocues, make sure you have practised first, so that you are not looking down and reading (as if a script). You need to scan, look up and speak, much as you do with cue cards.

ELEVATOR PITCHES AND SPEAKING TO CAMERA

Ready with your soundbites

- Create a doorstep challenge for yourself and have three points for why you should lead a team always ready at your fingertips. No more than a minute in length overall.

- Imagine an elevator pitch with a young recruit to your company and make them feel worthwhile, valued and welcome in a minute.

- Film yourself talking to camera and see if you look natural and authentic.

11.
DICTION, DELIVERY AND JARGON

Regional dialects

Something many people ask me is: 'will my foreign or regional dialect affect my chances of promotion?'. My reply is that a person's regional dialect is part of their culture, who they are and where they come from. It is individual to you and should be celebrated. Any company worth their professional salt won't discriminate against anyone for their accent. In Britain, for example, over the past 20 years, certain regional dialects are now considered particularly attractive and are increasingly in demand. Scottish accents, especially from Edinburgh, are popular, as well as southern Welsh and southern Irish.

There has also been a welcome shift in newscasters' voices. No longer is RP (received pronunciation or the

Queen's English) essential. Regional and foreign accents are now more commonly heard too, bringing a welcome diversity of voices to the media. Call centres like to use Scottish accents because they are deemed to be warm and friendly. Cheryl Cole (X Factor host and singer with Girls Aloud) has been voted the sexiest woman in the world and it seems her popularity is due partly to her Geordie accent from the North East.

Wherever you are from, your accent is part of your culture. We must celebrate the cultural differences in our backgrounds. Don't try to hide it, just speak clearly and with diction. A tip when thinking about diction is to remember that clarity of speech comes mainly from consonants, especially the final consonants, not vowels. For example, bath or path. Pronounce the p + th and the b + th. It is the vowel 'a' that changes sound in northern or southern dialects.

English as a second language

When you are presenting, it's also worth remembering that a large percentage of the people listening to you may not have English as their first language. Be respectful of this and avoid unnecessary jargon, acronyms or slang. Speak slowly, clearly and simply and all will benefit. As the speaker, it's our responsibility to make ourselves understood. Knowing who you are speaking to and acknowledging other people's needs and preferences is the way forward. Let's do our research, be sensitive and accommodate for differences.

Jargon

Different companies use an abundance of acronyms and abbreviations that are like a foreign language to everyone else. The technical industries especially revel in hoards of them. You are sitting in the audience at a presentation and you hear a list of letters and you spend the next ten minutes trying to work out what they are, by which time you have lost the thread of the presentation.

What does TfL mean to you? When I asked this question of a 70 strong group of business students at the University of Lancaster's management school, they replied: teacher of English as a foreign language (normally TEFL, again another acronym). For everyone in London, TfL is Transport for London, but why should overseas students studying at a northern university know that?

Many people say to me that they can use these acronyms as everyone in the audience has the same skills background and will be familiar, but there may be someone in the room who isn't an engineer, a lawyer or a technology expert. So that one person will be lost in the language. Allow me to give you an example. SOR has three separate meanings to my knowledge:

- 'statement of requirements' in project management
- 'schedule of rates' in construction
- 'system of record' as a data source

I remember when I first heard SOR, when working with people doing a master's degree in project management. I didn't dare ask at first (which is how most people react) because I thought I should know. It took courage to ask. I then discovered that it was a common abbreviation.

So the rule of thumb is that when you present you always give the full meaning of the acronym or abbreviation the first time you mention it, followed by the acronym which you can use for the rest of the presentation. For example, statement of requirements or SOR, which will be referred to as SOR throughout the rest of this presentation. You can only do this if you think it is fairly common knowledge with your audience. If in doubt, then continue to use the full description.

Company cultures

We experience cultural differences not just between nations but across companies as well; whether consciously or not, organizations all harbour attitudes which pool together to shape the company culture. These attitudes could be towards many things but might include age, gender, innovation, education, ethnicity, hierarchy, learning styles and so on. We can see a tech start-up that values ideas and initiative over university degrees, or a family-run business championing parents by offering generous maternity and paternity packages, while another company routinely hires people based on nepotism rather than merit. There's a smorgasbord of different cultures and practices out there, some good, some bad, but all of them are a reflection of the deeper attitudes of the company. What sort of companies do you like working for and doing business with? Our attitudes and values dictate our behaviours and people will unconsciously judge you by how you make them feel.

'I've learned that people will forget what you said, people will forget what you did, but people will never forget how you made them feel.'

Maya Angelou

There are significantly fewer female leaders in the top FTSE 100 companies (I believe six at the last count in 2019) and also fewer female public speakers than their male counterparts. The good news is that the number is growing all the time, there seems to be some momentum in these areas now that so many more women have built their confidence to be the leaders they want to be.

Exercises in clarity

- Check your next presentation for ease of comprehension. Could someone without native English or deep and specific industry knowledge understand you?

- What type of company culture do you want to help foster?

- Cut your abbreviations and acronyms from your next presentation.

- List the positive core attitudes that you hold, then think about how these could translate into actionable behaviours, either for you individually or for the wider team and organization.

12.
DIRECTIONS AND PROPS

Your presentation is now close to perfect in content and tone. What else could go wrong? Any one of a number of technical hitches, equipment malfunctions or missed cues could undo all your hard work.

You are now at the point where you have to try out your presentation for real. In this chapter, I am going to give you as many stage directions and technical tips as I can to help you be the best that you can be.

In theatre, it is when we do our technical rehearsals. What you will find is that when you do walk-throughs or microphone tests, it helps you become more comfortable and confident in what you are saying. For actors, it is just the same. In itself, a technical rehearsal can be mind-numbing and tiresome, but it gives you a chance to gain deeper familiarity with your text and your moves.

DIRECTIONS AND PROPS

Technical and logistical

Always have water handy in case you get a frog in the throat or experience a dry mouth. Opt for still over sparkling to avoid burping and hiccups.

If possible, check out the venue beforehand (a few hours or even a day ahead) to know where you'll be sitting before being called up to speak. Familiarizing yourself with the space and walking the route you'll take up to the stage can help you feel more comfortable when you come to do it live. Stand where you know you will speak from and run through your opening section.

If speaking without a microphone, check the acoustics and ask someone to stand right at the back to make sure you can be heard. If you are going to be miked up, then ask to have a soundcheck with the sound engineer before going on. Give yourself a little time to become comfortable wearing or holding the microphone and hearing your voice through the speakers. The less novelty you experience on the day the better.

Never speak from a loose sheet of A4. Why? It's highly distracting. Your natural adrenaline when speaking in front of an audience may cause your hand to shake, which will mean you now have a conspicuously trembling piece of paper drawing the attention of your audience, so they are now no longer fully listening to you. That quivering paper also suggests that you are nervous and, whether you are or not, it makes for an uncomfortable viewing experience. The empathetic listener wants your presentation to go well, and, in perceiving your nerves, will become nervous and worried for you. They will enjoy your presentation less and become less receptive to whatever message you are trying to deliver.

If you ever have to read a poem (at a wedding or a funeral, for example), and you haven't learned it off by heart, then print it in large, clear and generously spaced font, then attach it to something firm like a clipboard or piece of thick card. Practise with it until you are able to raise your head to speak rather than keeping your eyes down to read all the time. Hold it to the side of your body, so it's not blocking you from the audience. Choirs do the same, deliberately placing their music stands off centre to leave their bodies uncovered and thus create further connection with listeners.

Cue cards

If you need prompts, and most of us do, I highly recommend using cue cards. The aim is to write clear, concise reminders, which you can instantly make sense of, and that will help to keep your presentation flowing. Everyone's cue-card style is slightly different, and you will find what works best for

DIRECTIONS AND PROPS

you. Transcribing your entire presentation word for word though is not helpful. Remember these are prompts rather than a script.

Number each card in sequence clearly so you can easily get them back in order if they get muddled.

Use thick felt tip pen. Why? Because when you present you want to be able to scan read, which is not possible with thin, spidery biro.

Many people find it helpful using different coloured pens for different thoughts. For example, if you tend to speak quickly and are bad at pausing, write 'pause' in red wherever needed.

You can use your cards portrait or landscape, but try to hold them in just one hand and make them an extension of your gestures.

Avoid holding them with both hands or you risk looking like you're reading from a script in school assembly.

Here are three options you can try for managing your cue cards:

- Keep them in your hand all the time.

- Keep them in your pocket and pull them out in a pause if you feel the need of a reminder for your next part.

- Lay them out sequentially on a nearby table or lectern and use a pause in your speech to return to glance at them. This also gives the audience a chance to reflect on what you've just said.

When you use the cue card to remind yourself of the next thing you want to say, stop, look at the card, then look up to deliver the message.

Please don't speak down to the cue card or we will lose your eyes and eye contact is integral to a successful presentation.

The sequence we're aiming for is: scan, digest, look up, speak. Scan – digest – look up – speak.

Lecterns

If a lectern is provided, use it only for your cue cards and your glass of water. I know it can seem like the obvious place from which to stand and speak, and many of us do, as it offers a tempting comfort zone, a stronghold, but standing behind a table or lectern cuts us in half visually and puts a barrier between speaker and audience.

Subconsciously, your audience will detect this guarded behaviour, and the result is a distancing between you, as you appear less present, confident and accessible. This is especially relevant if you happen to be shorter; quite often we will see just a floating head and shoulders speaking and all the subtlety of body language is lost.

In order to optimize engagement and rapport with your audience, the body should be open and exposed. It can feel intimidating, I know. Establishing this practice though, will allow for the full spectrum and power of your presence to be communicated. If you have ever watched TED talks online, you will notice that all these world-class speakers share the ability to step out from behind the lectern and communicate with their whole bodies.

Phones in the workplace

Regardless of culture, one thing that is widely taken to be discourteous in business situations is the use of phones. Unless it is an emergency, looking at our phones during meetings or other people's presentations is disrespectful and shows we are not paying attention. It can be a common problem though, particularly when speaking to larger audiences and in auditoriums.

I was invited to speak by a multinational engineering firm at its annual conference in Washington DC. The venue was the renowned Mayflower Hotel, where inauguration balls for US presidents are usually hosted, and 1500 senior executives from around the world were attending.

The keynote speaker was the managing director, a lovely Scot, who called me to his room a few hours before he was due to go on stage, as he wanted a little help with his speech. Additionally, he had been asked to read some housekeeping that included reminding people to turn off their mobile phones. From each of our experiences we both knew that a passing announcement was unlikely to be effective, so we came up with the idea of relating the message back to the company's values and the rule of three.

When he came out on stage to begin the evening, he first asked the audience: 'do you think respect is an important value of our company? And what about listening to one another?'. The audience nodded and murmured assent. 'How do we show this in our behaviours? What does it say when we look at our phones when we are listening to a speaker or in a meeting with colleagues? Do you think that this behaviour shows respect and listening? Probably not.'

He went on to request that everyone please switch off their phones unless they had an emergency situation, in which case they were welcome to take the call outside the conference room. When it came to the speeches that night, I didn't see one phone come out and you could hear a pin drop.

DIRECTIONS AND PROPS

Time and manners

The mindful keeping of time is an essential consideration when preparing and delivering any presentation. If we're invited to speak for ten minutes, it's important we stick to it. Practice with a stopwatch beforehand and try to stay slightly under the allotted time. We often tend to ad lib a little more on the day or end up speaking for longer than we realize as we haven't practised aloud enough.

If you do come under time, the listener will love you: less is usually more, as it leaves them with some mental energy still in the tank. If you spill over the allotted time, your words may lose brevity and impact, and your polite audience can quickly become restless and distracted. Once our audience switches off, we may as well stop speaking.

Of course, it's not just the audience who suffers when we go over time. When speaking as part of a line-up, if we overrun, we are stealing the next speaker's time and could be throwing other elements of the event off course.

I'm reminded of a friend who worked for many years in event management running large, charity gala events. She told me that there were occasions when guest speakers (often celebrities) would jeopardize the whole project by getting lost in their own moment in the spotlight and failing to consider the event as a whole.

For example, it happened on occasion that over dinner, despite being briefed with precise timings (and subsequent flailing signals from off stage), some speakers would ramble on for 40 minutes or more instead of their allotted 20. This would of course have knock-on effects. She explained how it would push the live fundraising auction back, meaning the poor auctioneer now had to contend with a room full of guests, who, having been talked at for so long already, were too drunk to focus and completely disengaged. The prime money-making opportunity of the night suffered and the charity would lose out. The dinner service could also become severely delayed and it might be 11:00 pm before dessert was served. So everyone at the event and all the staff were kept there late.

It's unlikely that it was ever the culprit's intention to throw the night so off kilter and cause these repercussions. It is not a behaviour of malice, but of thoughtlessness or ego and a lack of self-awareness. No matter how big or small the speaking engagement is, we are part of a collaboration, a team effort that is always bigger than any one person and selfish behaviours do not go unnoticed by those around us.

My friend noted that the speakers who stood out (and she would happily invite back) were those who acted with consideration to the whole: observing timings, accommodating changes and always taking a moment to acknowledge the wider team of sound technicians, venue staff, fellow speakers and so on. Apparently, some of the loveliest names she had the pleasure of working with were Joanna Lumley, Stephen Fry and Rory Bremner, who engaged with everyone around them with warmth, humility and professionalism.

For actors, it is easy to see the commonalities between the stage and these events. Just like the theatre, events, parties, conferences and so on are a collaborative art. When I attended the Webber-Douglas Academy of Dramatic Art, if we were ever more than three minutes late to rehearsal, we were all sent home. The whole cast and crew suffered, which was mortifying for the late arrival.

Even when it may not be apparent exactly how our poor timekeeping could affect others, chances are that it will. Arrive punctually and speak for the time you've been given, and you are sure to be noted as a conscientious team player. Developing this respectful and cooperative attitude will serve you not only as a higher level speaker, but as a more rounded person, who people respect and enjoy working with.

Rehearsal exercises

- Try using cue cards as your prompts and not PowerPoint.

- Try stepping away from the lectern next time you are offered one and use it simply for your cue cards and water.

- Check your venue for acoustics beforehand.

- Time yourself speaking to ensure you are in the allotted time frame. Speak it out loud to the trees, your dog or your baby in real time.

13.
PERFORMING AS A LEADER

'Out of suffering have emerged the strongest souls; the most massive characters are seared with scars.'

Kahlil Gibran, *The Prophet*

Film can tell us much about how leaders perform when it really matters. Let us take two productions of Shakespeare's *Henry V* as an example. Some of you may remember that the morning before the battle of Agincourt, Henry himself made the speech:

> We few, we happy few, we band of brothers;
> For he today that sheds his blood with me
> Shall be my brother.

Henry here is sharing with his troops brotherly affection, to hold their love through the oncoming battle and give them strength to fight. Shakespeare himself highlighted the necessity of collaborative power no matter what rank you held. The army and the king need to work together to achieve success.

In the version made in 1989 with Kenneth Branagh in the title role, you will notice that he walks amongst his men before the battle, he touches them, he smiles at them, mentions the names, Bedford and Exeter, Warwick and Talbot, Salisbury and Gloucester, looking directly at them, making eye contact. They smile back with friendship. The atmosphere is calm and family like. He speaks with passion to raise their spirits, shows no obvious fear, but there is a humility of one who relies on his men to work together with him.

Now look at the 1944 film version with Laurence Olivier, a consummate actor, in the title role. The film was made expressly to raise the spirits of the soldiers, sailors, airmen and women, who had already been at war for five years. The film played an important role at the time and was successful. However, befitting the style of the time we see a declamatory performance, no smiling, no touching, no personal reference, but a more aloof style with a touch of haughtiness, devoid of humility.

Leadership styles have changed significantly since 1944. Theatre and film are collaborative arts and the crossover between leadership and the theatre has come closer and more interrelated in the intervening years.

It is those leaders in companies who always say good morning to their staff, those who remember the names of their colleagues, make eye contact, and who truly have time to listen, who are viewed as strong communicators. This doesn't have to take long, but it can be a daily or a weekly ritual where they drop by the desks of people in their company to check in and ask after their interests. Through the stories they hear from their people, the stories they listen to, they widen their lens and build credibility and empathy, making them better public speakers equipped to lead with truth and sincerity. Behaviours like these demonstrate humility and make us more approachable. Better leaders try to foster a universal approach, a worldliness through which to show texture in communication and an awareness of others around us.

At its heart, I think the essence of leadership is to hold strong values and live and work by them. Whatever those values are, they need to be obvious to those around us both in our words and actions. As Virginia Satir, the noted American author and psychotherapist, says: 'How you express yourself visually, vocally and verbally reflects you and your belief structure. When you talk, the words, feeling and body must be in harmony.'

Powerful, inspiring and sincere leaders always present

with body language, intention and the words in harmony. Barack Obama generally comes across as sincere as he speaks from the heart, usually without notes. He knows what he wants to say and his core values are embedded in his delivery.

Upon graduating from Harvard Law School, Obama turned down the opportunity of working in a New York law practice and chose instead to work in Chicago supporting the underprivileged on a developing communities project. That experience, along with his upbringing, has helped give him insight into the human condition. It took him years of trial and error and talking and listening to everyday folks to understand the needs of his people.

We want to see and feel our leaders' sincerity. This is why what we do, and not only what we say, is so important in public speaking and leadership communication. All of our daily, micro communications and interactions matter just as much as the minutes spent on stage delivering a talk. We need to see that leaders actually do what they promise. We need to see action not just words.

The focus on leadership values only intensifies in the face of economic downturn, internal corporate struggle or political upheavals. I was asked by a FTSE 100 company to attend one of their regional offices in Manchester to help work on a proposal for an account that would bring them more than £1 million. I sat at a table with all the people who would be involved with the proposal and the presentation. The leader of the proposal, Bill, walked in and said briskly to the group: 'so how are we going to run this bid?'.

Everyone looked at the ground or the desk because they had all been put on the spot, no one spoke. He then said: 'alright, why don't you (pointing to Jo), be responsible for the IT input and why don't you, Sheena, handle the audit issues,' and so on.

When he had finished doling out a role for everybody, still no one spoke and he swiftly left the room. As soon as he was gone, people started talking and complaining. Bill had dictated to them what they should do and had not allowed their creativity or motivation to blossom.

Later that day I was asked by the head of that branch to talk to Bill about how he had become over-assertive and aggressive in the handling of his staff. Why me? Because I was an external consultant and no one in the office would dare give Bill this feedback for fear of losing their promotions or even their jobs.

I did talk to Bill about the fact that he seemed to have lost touch with his team and he took the feedback well. We discovered together that one of the reasons was that his office had been moved away from his team, who remained on the ground floor of the building, while his office had been relocated to the fourth floor. As a result, he did not see his people on a daily basis anymore and he had not taken the time to go and visit them, even for occasional, informal chats. As a result, his team felt a distance from him and simply hadn't felt comfortable or confident enough to come up with ideas on the spot in that meeting.

There is a reason that my theatre work wove itself seamlessly into training and facilitating in business. Theatre is teamwork. So is good leadership. Every person in a company is important: from the person who delivers the post to the senior consultant. They are all part of the team and without a good dose of humility, true leadership success will be elusive. The standard we must hold ourselves to is a success beyond the financial bottom line; sustainable success, a success that takes responsibility for the fulfilment and wellbeing of all staff, contributes positively to its community and earns trust, satisfaction and loyalty from its customers.

Leadership in presentation is like leadership in life. To have credibility with our audience we must have integrity in our speech and strive to embody our values.

'Success is a consequence and must not be the goal.'

Gustav Flaubert

Exercises in leadership

Consider these questions and write down your answers:

- What values do you admire and like to see in a leader?

- Think of an actual leader you admire.

- What values are important to you in your own life?

- What actions could you take that embody your values?

14.
BUSINESS THEATRE

So far we have drawn on theatrical experiences to support the presentations you are making in settings with which you are broadly familiar. But what happens if we take you into the theatre itself?

Here's how one of my partners, Nichols, strategic change advisors and a creative agency, describes the experiences it helps to create:

> Theatre has always been a captivating way of sharing stories. We embrace this and use creative business theatre to convey messages, share ideas and raise business consciousness ... theatre allows you to explore, discover and express your key messages and ideas with movement, imagination and play.

Let's see if we can unpack those skills that lie behind how a theatrical production captivates an audience or gives a cast the confidence to perform. Allow me first to tell you the story of how we developed a creative germ into a play that could entertain and inform a business audience, more used to the day-to-day realities of schedules and budgets.

Inspire and entertain

A few years ago, I was charged with producing a theatrical analogy, a play, to highlight the challenges in complex projects. As always, such productions are a collaborative art. A piece of theatre or film or dance cannot happen without a large group of people backstage and out front working together. Good theatre tells stories to which its audience can relate.

Our drama was set around the disciplines of managing programmes and projects. We were asked to think of moment at which they shaped our history. We chose Elizabeth I and her fight against the Spanish Armada with her own fleet of ships. Most people in Britain recognize her as a character, as well as Sir Francis Drake and William Shakespeare. We adopted a style that was close to the BBC's historical comedy, *Blackadder*.

Scenarios in project management always involve the client, the user and the project manager. In this instance, the client was Elizabeth I; the user was Sir Francis Drake; and the poor project manager was a downtrodden cousin of the bard called Colin Shakespeare from Birmingham.

The project was commissioned as a co-venture by the Major Projects Association with Nichols and was first shown at its annual general meeting. It was such a success that we were asked to do it for Rolls-Royce in Bristol, for Nichols at Haberdasher's Hall, then at the Queen Elizabeth II Conference Centre for the Association of Project Management, and, ultimately, for the annual conference of a large international company, Aecom, at the Mayflower Hotel in Washington DC.

Each was well received and better than a PowerPoint presentation any day of the week. Like all good theatre, it worked on several levels: it told a story, it was highly entertaining and it was relevant to the audience. It highlighted that clients (like Elizabeth I) never have enough money for the project that they want built. In our little play, the queen tried to persuade Sir Francis Drake, who ultimately was going to combat the Spanish, to pillage and rob their existing ships to fund the new ones being built for her. That bit went down a storm. The poor shipbuilder (or project manager) played by Colin Shakespeare was given directives from both the queen and Sir Francis Drake, yet was never given any money to complete the project.

BUSINESS THEATRE

Every project manager in the audience related to his situation, because most people, including the Norwegian and Swedish workforce at Rolls-Royce, know the story of Elizabeth I and have read some Shakespeare at school. All historical facts were completely true and well researched; the costumes and wigs were of a high standard; and the professional actors well cast for their roles. They all excelled in comic timing and worked seamlessly together. Acting is reacting.

The team who created this piece of theatre worked tirelessly and collaboratively to achieve the end. First, the scriptwriter had to work closely with the company, Nichols and the MPA, so that the key messages were prominent within the script. The producer had to work with the designers, as well as the director, and liaise with the company to make sure the project was going to be on time and on budget.

I hope you can see how this creation not only in content, but also in production, matches the construction and delivery of a major project. It was entertaining, engaging and enlightening. Project and programme managers were able to see themselves within the piece, recognizing where they could go wrong and how powerful communication is the answer to managing a successful project. They also enjoyed seeing how they have reason to complain about clients who don't pay on time and how diplomatic they have to be in order to get the project completed on budget, even if they don't have one.

Your own performance

How could you and your company set about creating your own business theatre? The first thing you need is a concept for the production whether from an original idea or from a recognized script; an objective of what you want your play to say to your clients.

Then you need to find a scriptwriter. You may have someone in your company who could step in; if not, try *Contacts*, which is a journal produced annually by the theatrical trade organization, Spotlight (www.spotlight.com/contacts).

Once you have your script, the director is the all-important person to realize your vision. Just as a good leader will have an overall vision for a company so a director will have one for a play. The director, like a good leader, will encourage and ask questions of actors that allow them to blossom and find their own way of telling the story.

For example, a director will ask their actors: 'what does your character feel now?' or 'what does your character want to achieve now?'. In the same way a supportive and positive leader of a company will ask a team: 'how do you feel about this project?' or 'what do think would be the best way forward?'. Poor directors in theatre are those who tell you where to go on the stage or what to do, rather than letting you find the move or journey yourself.

Beyond comfort zones

Pantomime offers a different way of using theatre within the world of organizations and teams. Impact International used these skills in developing the under-19 England cricket team. Many of these young men had never ventured outside their comfort zones, as their whole life had been dedicated to cricket from as young as three or four years-old.

We were asked to teach them the quintessential skills of pantomime and come up with a script. On this occasion, it was *Cinderella*. As we know in traditional British panto, the two ugly sisters are played by men dressed in outrageous frocks. Imagine the reaction from these young cricketers when we proposed this idea.

They were then shown an advert from the local newspaper stating that there would be a performance of their pantomime the following afternoon at 3.30 pm to 120 schoolchildren. There is nothing like a date and a time to focus minds. The group had to choose their roles, whether as performer, sound technician, props buyer, costume designer, lighting technician, director or producer. All these roles are necessary in a live production.

It was wonderful to see shy introverted young men suddenly spring to life, playing a dame, going around charity shops seeking wands and strange bits of costume, and opening up their creative thoughts to stage design. Some of these young cricketers had never been away from home before.

The result was that the cricket coaches felt the young men had matured through the process, taken personal responsibility for their actions and travelled well beyond their comfort zones. So what did their production of a pantomime teach them?

Ultimately, and most importantly, their pantomime was a collaboration of ideas and actions to make a cohesive (if a little ragged around the edges) show. Nobody could work alone. In each of their unfamiliar roles, they all depended on each other.

Cricket is a team game. This exercise helped these cricketers get to know one another and work seamlessly together. The following year, these skills contributed to a series of outstandingly good results in matches round the world.

BUSINESS THEATRE

Winning performances

It is easier to use pantomime to train teams and encourage collaboration. A script for a straight play brings more constraints. Stock characters in pantomime are familiar to British audiences, who can feel comfortable that there will be a happy outcome. It is fun and neither the actors, the designer nor the director are required to think too deeply. So, although these cricketers were outside their comfort zones as performers, the idea was uncomplicated. In this way, your team, and not professional actors, can achieve their goals too.

Here we have two completely different forms of business theatre. The first with a script using professional actors, as in *The Armada*, to promote visionary ideas and entertain clients; the second using pantomime to encourage teams to work outside their comfort zones and understand how they can use their strengths to work alongside each other in whatever guise.

In either format, theatre stretches us as performers and presenters in unexpected ways and puts our skills to the test, leaving a lasting impression and sense of achievement among those who were involved in the production and those who saw it happen live.

Exercises in business theatre

- Think how your company could endorse and promote a business theatre experience.

- Create your own small theatre scenes with all your team playing parts. Possibly use company stories.

- How could you create a teambuilding and communication experience by using theatre techniques?

15.
CORNERSTONES AND COMPETENCE

'Tell the truth and you'll have nothing to remember.'

Mark Twain

Oh, how right he was. When you tell your truth it is there in your heart and you have no need to remember it. If you tell an untruth, how difficult it is to remember.

In this book, I hope I have revealed to you what I see as the three cornerstones of engaging public speaking:

- **Storytelling.** Disclosure, pathos, silent connection, rapport. Let people find a bit of themselves in your stories. Harness the power of emotion to become relatable and build connection with your audience.

- **Authenticity.** Your truth is what's important. Be who you are. Use your unique strengths. If you play a role in life or in presentation, we are well tuned as humans to pick up on it and mistrust. Trust is essential in the building of healthy relationships both personal and corporate.

- **Self-awareness.** Knowing who you are and how you come over to others. Pay attention to the effect you have on others, adjust and respond accordingly and invite feedback that will help you grow. Self-awareness, and not self-consciousness, gives us the confidence to be who we are and not who we think we ought to be. Being certain of who you are and being comfortable in your own skin is key to relaxed, confident communication. Without self-awareness we cannot be good communicators.

At the close of all my courses, I always ask each delegate for a 'burning learning'. This is one single idea, a light-bulb moment of recognition or learning that they have gathered whilst being totally present on the programme. The answers vary hugely:

- 'I found the breathing and relaxation exercises really

useful because they calmed me down and reduced my panic level.'

- 'I found the simple structure and the rule of three you suggested invaluable.'

- 'I actually feel myself beginning to enjoy presenting.'

- 'I am not as bad at it as I thought.'

Let's look at what you may have learnt. Here is a potted version of what you need to think about when you begin preparing for your next talk or presentation.

- Think of the overall objective of what you want or need to say.

- Then think of a story around it.

- Decide what are the three key messages and possibly find three stories to illustrate them.

- Talk through your ideas with a colleague or coach so they become clear in your mind.

- Think of your communication strengths and use them.

- Who is your audience and what will engage them?

- Find a cracking opening and close.

Done. There seems to be a simplicity to this, and to a great extent there is: public speaking isn't rocket science and, as we've explored, there exists a range of tactics and tips for getting a decent handle on it quite quickly. But we should also recognize when there is self-developmental work to be done. I personally don't believe there is a magic, one-size-fits-all formula or right way to present. Any overly prescriptive training models that make such claims are usually counter-productive in helping people actually become the best speakers they could be. My approach is that of ongoing self-discovery and confidence-building to be able to share your natural self in all situations.

In my courses, I often begin by discussing the four stages of competence, which apply to the attainment of any skill, including presenting. Here, I will close with it.

- **Unconscious incompetence**: unaware of a skill you lack.

- **Conscious incompetence**: aware that you lack a skill.

- **Conscious competence**: actively working at a skill, although it requires a lot of thought and hard work.

- **Unconscious competence**: in the moment/present. So skilled that you no longer even have to think about it.

In the context of public speaking, to be unconsciously competent is to speak naturally as your confident and authentic self. That's all there is to it, though the time scale for this progression will vary for each of us: it is a personal evolution with no right or wrong. Which phase are you currently in with your public speaking? Whatever your current level of competency, with a sincere willingness to learn, some practice and patience, you will enjoy growth and achieve your goals.

What is the path that a motivational speaker might take? How can you in fact arrive at the level of a TED talk or its equivalent for your industry?

Let me share with you the story of Lisa, a bright young woman I worked with, who went from being a nervous, unsure, hesitant presenter to becoming a smiling, confident, articulate speaker who could express herself fluently and with passion:

When I started, public speaking would make me physically shake, make me feel like my voice was wobbling and breaking. I would get those feelings you get before you faint, where everything goes a bit quiet and dark, and time goes by in a blur. My main goal was to 'survive it' and the concept of actually enjoying it was laughable. I would never volunteer to speak and would be inclined to say no if asked. It was an ordeal.

I have experienced a remarkable change in how I feel about public speaking, and, I hope, in how I come across when I do it.

The overwhelming nerves I used to feel now only hit me for a few seconds right at the beginning, and the techniques to manage them have been really effective, even if just giving me something else to do which takes my mind off it.

The feeling of only being able to aim for survival has been replaced with something that could almost be classified as enjoyment, though I have more work to do to reach that pinnacle.

The relief I used to feel after 'getting through

it' has been replaced by a sense of pride and achievement.

Lisa from the Nichols Group was nominated for the prestigious award, Every Woman in Transport, by Costain and Skanska, two construction engineering companies. She had to go through a nerve-wracking filmed interview before she was selected. Then the following month, she presented at the Major Projects Association when they had a conference on embracing diversity where she gave an affirming talk on 'The Colour of Competence'.

As a woman of mixed race herself, she was able to talk compellingly through contentious issues like unconscious bias and positive discrimination. Lisa won the award and commented that she found that the process of sharing ideas, making them clear in her mind, then structuring them together with me, allowed her to talk conversationally and authentically, seemingly off the cuff, without the need for copious notes. That is unconscious competence and Lisa is certainly an example of someone who has achieved the rewarding transformation from conscious incompetence to the prized stage of unconscious competence through her diligence and application of the techniques we've covered together in this book.

TED status

Allow me to share with you one final story of a man who has reached TED status. I was asked by a facilitator I met in the United States to go to Guguletu, a township in Cape Town, South Africa to work with a man called Thembile.

Thembile had suffered a series of strokes at the age of 39, which weren't treated for 18 days, leaving him incapacitated with his left side severely paralyzed and his speech almost incomprehensible. He was married with three children. He had been an experiential educator, leading management and executives into difficult terrain and up mountains. He had been extremely fit. It took him 18 months to walk again after his strokes. He then started an artisan bakery in the back yard of his humble home with the help of BreadRev. He had to find the resilience and courage to heal, control his emotions which were near the surface at all times and yet still work. His ultimate passion was to be a motivational speaker, to share his story. That's where I came in.

We spent two weeks working nine hours a day together. I spent two hours using voice and breathing exercises to improve his speech, which I brought from the acting world. The rest of the time, Thembile poured forth with a string of incredible stories about his life before and after the strokes. He had grown up during apartheid and suffered all its horrors and deprivations: little schooling, poor accommodation, segregation and poverty. Together we structured these stories.

Towards the end of our time together, we did a dress rehearsal for family and friends of the five presentations on which we had worked. It was programmed for a Sunday afternoon when everybody would be available. However, at 3:00 pm when we should have started, only two people had arrived. They drifted in over the next hour chatting in a relaxed way, so we started an hour late. All through the presentation, people were talking, horns were honking, babies were crying, his mother had an argument with the lady next door over the bougainvillea and his drunken brother cried all the way through with big tears rolling down his face. It was all very African: chaotic, colourful and full of life. Flexibility was the key.

However, two days later we did a corporate presentation to various non-governmental organizations, the head of the South African Chamber of Baking, local journalists, the local pastor of the church, people from retirement homes, local bankers and small business leaders. A real mix.

It was delivered in the open sun in Thembile's front yard beside his garage where the bakers were making the artisan bread. Everybody there had an opportunity to knead some dough (fold, tuck, turn) and make a cheese breadstick.

Thembile also demonstrated his one-handed mixing and kneading art form. As he said, he was the only one-handed baker at bakery school. His sense of self-deprecating humour touched everyone's hearts.

By the end of the presentation, most people were in tears and profoundly moved. He spoke sincerely of how he had changed his life to thinking of others and he was happy to be able to serve the community in any way he could. He was asked to apply for a peace scholarship at Hartford University, he has already given several talks to the Wheelchair Warriors, to the local church and colleges, and to the Bakery Association of South Africa.

He has become inspirational to the other people within his community because of his determination to cope with his adversity and using bread baking as a lifeline has made him a role model to his contemporaries and the youth in Guguletu and beyond. Recently he got a place at Stellenbosch University to study business skills. He is building his business, but it is his public speaking that has brought him recognition throughout Cape Town and South Africa. Adversity brings opportunity.

I wanted to share this story with you because if Thembile can become a motivational speaker with all his disadvantages then so can you. So what did he do? He:

- worked hard;

- was completely open;

- engaged by sharing his life stories, both good and bad;

- worked on posture and vocal abilities;

- listened to his teachers and helpers;

- was always seeing his experience from the audience viewpoint;

- and was completely himself – authentic.

Ultimately, practice and experience along with self-awareness and empathy will make you a better communicator. However, the mistakes, turmoil and tears along the way also give us a better understanding of both ourselves and others, so don't be deterred by any hiccups. If we work on the three pillars of communication, and take into account that passion and enthusiasm are key to engagement, we have lift off.

So, my wish for you on the day of your presentation is simply to feel calm, prepared and completely confident in who you are and what you want to say, so you can be at your best, be authentic. I believe wholeheartedly that you can do it.

Final tips for speaking success

- Warm up your voice and body before speaking. Breathe deeply three times.

- Know your strengths.

- Speak in the moment.

- No more than three key messages.

- Keep your own little black book of creativity which is filled with anecdotes and stories.

APPENDIX 1
TEN INSPIRING ARTICLES, TALKS AND IDEAS

1. How sharing your vulnerability with your audience can build understanding and empathy: 'The Power of Vulnerability', a TED talk on personal storytelling by Brené Brown at https://www.ted.com/talks/brene_brown_on_vulnerability#t-764183.

2. How achievement of a physical challenge is not achieved without humility towards the environment: 'My mind-Shifting Everest swim', an engagingly delivered TED talk by Lewis Pugh at https://www.ted.com/talks/lewis_pugh_s_mind_shifting_mt_everest_swim.

3. Kindness in a leader is paramount: 'You are not so kind as you used to be', a letter by Clementine Churchill to her husband Winston Churchill, number 37, *Letters of Note*, compiled by Shaun Usher, ISBN: 978 1 78211 2235.

4. Refusal of Nick Cave, the Australian rock musician, to accept an MTV music award as he felt that competition is an indignity. However, he does it with courtesy grace and charm: 'My muse is not a horse', a letter by Nick Cave, number 30, *Letters of Note*, compiled by Shaun Usher, ISBN: 978 1 78211 2235.

5. In Dr Maya Angelou's ten rules for success, her delivery style is a model of calm pace, humour, passion and gravitas, while her wisdom is to be savoured: https://www.youtube.com/watch?v=iU46Lv4jVAw&t=226s.

6. A US president shares facing fear and failure. Leaders take note: 'The Man in the Arena', speech by Theodore Roosevelt, taken from *Citizen in a Republic*.

7. The action of a leader that makes the most difference is setting a personal example: *The Leadership Challenge*, Kouzes & Posner (especially Chapter 4, 'Set the Example').

8. Deborah Francis White, a stand-up comic who includes her audience in her talk, points out good, and not so good, forms of presentation in a humourous way: 'Charisma versus Stage Fright', a TED talk by

Deborah Francis White at https://www.youtube.com/watch?v=IdJbJMUFzZA.

9. Malala Yousafzali's acceptance speech for her Nobel Peace Prize is a good example of clarity, repetition, self-deprecation and considered pace with pause: https://www.nobelprize.org/prizes/peace/2014/yousafzai/lecture/.

10. Why EQ matters more than IQ; emotional quotient is essential for engaging public speaking: Emotional Intelligence, Daniel Goleman, published by: Bantam, ISBN: 055380491X.

APPENDIX 2
WARM-UP ROUTINES

A great learning that I brought from theatre to the world of business is preparation. What do I mean by that? Before a performance, especially on opening night when nerves are heightened, I walk the space and check the acoustics, asking a fellow actor to stand at the back of the auditorium to see if they can hear me adequately. If you can't be heard, the audience will switch off.

I check all my props are in place: maybe a glass of water on a table or a hat and coat ready to put on during the scene. The stage manager will have set them already, but I will check again.

I do my vocal warm-up with some humming and tongue-twisters, and my physical warm-up, stretching, flopping over and re-building my spine, then most importantly 3 x 3 sets of deep breaths counting form 1 to 10, 1 to 15 and 1 to 20 on exhalation.

I will continue to do diction exercises to keep my mind

from going into fear mode. The more you can keep your mind clear with breathing exercises, warming up your speech organs (tongue, teeth, soft palate, hard palate and alveolar ridge at the back of your upper teeth), the less the fear will attack you.

I have used this practice routine with many speakers and presenters. If you are prepared, if you know where everything is, including your slides and cue cards, if you have checked the room, the timing and the microphone, and, most importantly, if you have warmed up your voice and body, then you will feel more confident and be ready to give your best.

Everyone loves one exercise that I brought with me from drama school back in the 1970s. My voice teacher, Hilary Liddell, taught us the following ditty or 'diaphragmatic hoot', which is fun, makes people laugh, uses the breathing techniques and sharpens the diction. Say:

- cup of coffee (twice);

- cheese and biscuits (twice);

- apple and blackberry (twice).

PERSONAL PRESENCE

Now breathe and then say:

- fish and chips (three times);

- SOUPPPP (expelling all the air in your diaphragm and crisply delineating that final P of soup).

ACKNOWLEDGEMENTS

I always feel when I look at the acknowledgment section of a book that I want to know more about those people mentioned. I am curious. So, dear reader, I am going to tell you about the host of people who supported me through this challenging and soul-searching journey.

Back in 2009 my dear brother Piers had died and I was bereft. My personal assistant at the time, Harriet Mackie, suggested I write a book about my work to take my mind off my grief and give me focus. Week by week, she encouraged me through a synopsis of chapters and the basic format. She then became a producer in theatre, so the book was sidelined.

Two years ago, I picked it up again through the encouragement of my daughter, Hannah. This time, ten years on I had a different motivation: to write a book that could help people be the best of themselves. Hannah saw that. At the suggestion of her and her partner, Charles, another young whizz kid, Cam Minden, worked alongside me, coaxing and listening. As I am a person who feels at home with the spoken word, I found putting the tone, emphasis and engagement into writing that fully expressed my meaning a trial. With patience and encouragement, Cam was able to translate some of those spoken words onto paper. She gave me the shove I needed. Once my momentum was sparked, I was able to take off.

Then I had the most extraordinary luck to be introduced to Adam Jolly, my publisher, through Sara Render a dear friend from the business world. Adam had faith in me and encouraged me with positive support and kindness although at the same time making suggestions for extra chapters. The book was only 12 chapters when I contacted him. He soothed my anxious soul, allowed for my creativity to blossom and was always there at the end of the phone, suggesting, guiding and saying things like 'terrific' or 'that works'. Then his designer Chantel Barnett put the icing on the cake with the apt and delicate cover design: the chrysalis of the butterfly opening and emerging, flying to success and being itself in all its glory.

Ultimately this book would not have happened without my dear clients who employed me, paid me, have remained loyal and are now friends, Dave, Kathryn, Frances, Andrew, Verity, Tessa, Sara, Andy, Aman, Janie, Mark, Gary, Sascha,

ACKNOWLEDGEMENTS

Jonathan, Bruce, Tim, Mike and Lisa.

The often unsung heroes of my courses are the IT people who can always fix whatever I need whether it's the camera link to the screen or my computer or printer. I thank you, especially Terry and Colin.

I cannot leave this page without mentioning my family: Brigit who proofread all the chapters meticulously; Gwen who has both filmed me and helped with the machinations of social media; Hannah who has supported me all the way; and the rest of my family who have been somewhat surprised but also enlightened by my perseverance. And my dear supportive friends like Anna, Sue, Lucy, Helen, Jenny, Hayley, Deb, Katy, Calandra, Amy and Charles who raised my flagging spirits and spurred me on.

Over the years whilst coaching and facilitating, I have learned from my clients and students probably even more than they have learnt from me. I have also grown as a person and want to pass on that learning. As Alan Bennett said in *The History Boys*: 'Pass the parcel. That's sometimes all you can do. Take it, feel it, and pass it on. Not for me, not for you, but for someone, somewhere, one day. Pass it on, boys. That's the game I want you to learn. Pass it on.'

www.ingramcontent.com/pod-product-compliance
Lightning Source LLC
Chambersburg PA
CBHW020534080526
44583CB00013B/854